"Sissy Goff is unquestionably the expert in helping young women identify their strengths and areas of need. Sissy helps them shape their days
and their thoughts and therefore their futures. She is a gift to any family
raising a young woman in our culture and our time."

—Annie F. Downs, bestselling author and host
of the *That Sounds Fun* podcast

"This book was born out of a strongly felt need to address the anxiety
that many girls are facing today. In this book Sissy will take your hand,
speak the truth, and equip you with the tools you need to navigate your
way through the stormy seas of worry and anxiety. *Brave* is a timely gift.
Don't miss it."

—Ellie Holcomb, Dove Award–winning singer/songwriter

"As someone who struggles with anxiety, I am very thankful for this book.
It made me feel like Sissy was right there, sitting and talking with me. I
related to all of her examples, and it made me feel not so alone knowing
that other girls would be reading this and relating to it as well. This book
will be something I forever hold close to my heart. I hope other girls can
feel as thankful for Sissy as I do."

—Hallie, 13

"This book confirms what I've always known: Sissy has the ability to really
understand me! As a teenage girl who struggles with ADHD and anxiety,
Sissy's words encourage me and help me feel not so alone. Balancing
funny with serious, she makes talking about hard stuff not so daunting.
I know other girls will connect with this book and it will help them too!"

—Sydney, 14

"Throughout high school I have found myself struggling many times. I
felt the need to change myself to fit in and be liked. I felt anxious all the
time because I lost myself in trying to be everything I wasn't. Through
the ten years I've known Sissy, she has planted so much in my mind, and
it's all wrapped up in this book. The reminder that I'm not the only one

dealing with anxiety has helped me be not only happier with myself but a better friend to others."

—Eleanor, 17

"This book made me feel good to know that I wasn't alone in having worries. It was a great perspective on seeing how God can lead us through our worries and our anxiety."

—Piper, 13

"I love this book because it feels like Sissy really connects with me and is having a conversation with me. It is important to know that you are not the only one who deals with worry and anxiety. Don't let the Worry Monster get under your skin! God is always in control!"

—Kaitlyn, 13

"Sissy explained the parts of my anxiety that I've never been able to articulate. Being able to pull out the book and hear Sissy's insightful tips in the exact moment that I was feeling anxious was so helpful. This book is a game changer!"

—Catherine, 16

"I recommend this book to any teenage girl who struggles with any type of worry. This book shows you that it is okay to worry and that you aren't alone."

—Ella, 17

"Sissy has helped me through seasons of anxiety and fear and has been a rock in my life. This book is just like sitting in her office and feeling the safety that led me to overcome my anxiety. I know this book will help so many who, like me, were stuck and now are free."

—Seanna, 16

Brave

Brave

A Teen Girl's Guide to Beating Worry and Anxiety

Sissy Goff, MEd, LPC-MHSP

BETHANY HOUSE

a division of Baker Publishing Group
Minneapolis, Minnesota

Published by Bethany House Publishers
11400 Hampshire Avenue South
Bloomington, Minnesota 55438
www.bethanyhouse.com

Bethany House Publishers is a division of
Baker Publishing Group, Grand Rapids, Michigan

Printed in the United States of America

ISBN 978-0-7642-3839-0 (paperback)
ISBN 978-0-7642-3908-3 (casebound)
ISBN 978-1-4934-3163-2 (ebook)

Some names and recognizable details have been changed to protect the privacy of those who have shared their stories for this book.

The information in this book is intended solely as an educational resource, not a tool to be used for medical diagnosis or treatment. The information presented is in no way a substitute for consultation with a personal health care professional. Readers should consult their personal health care professional before adopting any of the suggestions in this book or drawing inferences from the text. The author and publisher specifically disclaim all responsibility for any liability, loss, or risk, personal or otherwise, which is incurred as a consequence, directly or indirectly, of the use of and/or application of any of the contents of this book.

Cover design by Dan Pitts

Interior illustrations on pages 17, 82, 84, 137, and 138 by Connie Gabbert.
Illustration on page 54 is based on Shutterstock image 588235892 by AVA Bitter.
Illustration on page 99 is based on Shutterstock image 102371905 by mhatzapa.
Illustration on page 161 is based on Shutterstock image 12619393 by olkapooh.
The Feelings Chart on page 189 was designed by Katie Plunkett. Used by permission. No reproductions allowed.

21 22 23 24 25 26 27   7 6 5 4 3 2

I think of faith as a kind of whistling in the dark because,
in much the same way, it helps to give us courage
and to hold the shadows at bay . . . to demonstrate,
if only to ourselves, that not even the dark can quite overcome
our trust in the ultimate triumph of the Living Light.

—*Frederick Buechner*

I have had the tremendous privilege of bearing witness to the whistling of thousands of girls in my almost thirty years as a counselor at Daystar Counseling Ministries. They have taught me, and their parents with them, what it looks like to truly live out this idea—this force—this blessed hope of bravery. This book is written for them, the girls and young women who have allowed me to sit with them in their stories and hear them whistle with strength, with beauty, and with a buoyant hope. Light wins every time. Thanks for leading the charge and being reminders of what it looks like to take heart, live brave, and whistle.

Contents

To the Parent Who Bought This Book

First of all, thank you. If you bought this book, my guess is you have a worrier, or you're worried that you have a worrier. I truly believe this book will help. Second, if you're *really* worried that you have a worrier, I suggest you grab a copy of *Raising Worry-Free Girls*. Here's why:

When my publisher first approached me about writing a book for girls on worry and anxiety, my immediate response was, "Only if you'll let me write one for parents too." Anxiety is not just a childhood epidemic in America today. It's also a parenting epidemic. If you struggle with anxiety, your child is up to seven times more likely to struggle with it herself.[1] A few more interesting facts: Most kids go two years before receiving any kind of help for their anxiety, and anxiety left untreated usually gets worse.[2] By the way, that's most of the bad news in *Raising Worry-Free Girls*. The rest of it is filled with good news that can help you and the worried girl you love, whatever her age.

Anxiety is tricky because it often doesn't look like anxiety. For younger girls, it can look more like manipulation and anger. As girls get older, it morphs into type A behavior or perfectionism.

It also looks like the child who loves control. The source of worry morphs over time as well, so it's easy to think the signs of anxiety were part of a phase because as soon as you start to notice how much she's worried about being away from you, it stops. A few months or years later, though, it emerges as worry about flying on airplanes or throwing up or any other unrelated topic. And the whac-a-mole game of parenting a child with anxiety begins. My guess is that if you have a teenager who is prone to worry, she's been that way for quite some time. It's undoubtedly enough to make you anxious, if you weren't already.

In this book I have outlined a few guidelines for her. My hope is that reading *Brave*, for her, will be much like sitting in my counseling office at Daystar. Obviously, I'm not in person with her, although I wish I were. But many of the same guidelines still apply—for her and for you.

The most important guideline is confidentiality. Not for her. She's welcome to talk to whomever she likes. I certainly hope she talks about her worries with you. In fact, I'll encourage that often throughout this book. The confidentiality clause is for you. I can't tell you how many times over the years of counseling girls I've heard a parent say something like "She left her journal out in the den because she really wanted me to read it." Teenagers are forgetful. Have you noticed how many things she leaves out? This book will only help if she's honest in what she writes, and that honesty will only happen if she believes you won't look through this book when she's at school. I know you want to help, but I recommend that you let this be her space. Every teenager needs space to process her emotions.

So here are your main guidelines:

1. Give her space to process.
2. The work is hers, not yours. Sorry—it sounds a little harsh, I know. You will also be tempted—and I would imagine have been tempted a lot over the years—to rescue her. In fact, the two most common strategies for dealing

with anxiety are escape and avoidance, according to cognitive therapy experts David Clark and Aaron Beck.[3] I don't mean you avoiding her, but you helping her escape and avoid whatever is making her anxious. If you have done those things, I have every confidence it was with the best of intentions. The problem is that neither strategy actually helps. The definition of anxiety I came up with in *Raising Worry-Free Girls* is this: "Anxiety always involves an overestimation of the problem and an underestimation of herself."[4] For her to work through her fear, she'll have to do the thing that scares her. I'm going to give her a lot of tools in these pages. She is capable. The work is hers.

3. Ask her open-ended questions about her work from time to time. Teenagers shut down when they feel like their parents are interrogating them (moms, I'm not pointing the finger specifically at you, but . . .). Don't ask her about it every day. Give her space to process. But every so often, ask her how it's going. What does she think of the book? What's one thing she's learned recently? I tell parents that breezy is the best posture when it comes to teenagers. Act breezy. If you care more than she does, she'll likely care less—on purpose.

4. Give her time to answer. She may not answer you right away. She may have to think about it. That's okay. Again, give her time and space to process.

5. Be aware of what you reinforce. Whatever you pay the most attention to as a parent is what's most reinforced. Pay more attention to her courage than her anxiety. Praise her for her bravery. Call out any time you see strength in her. Connect with her around what she can do and how she is capable, rather than the times she isn't or does her best to communicate to you that she's not. I have had teenage girls tell me that their moms are most nurturing when they have panic attacks. Be aware of what you're attending to the most.

6. When all else fails, offer empathy and questions. Empathy is always a good place to start with teenagers. It's hard to be a teenage girl in today's world—yes, harder than it was for us. It means a great deal to her when she knows that you see that. Empathize, and then ask questions. "That sounds hard. What do you think would help?" "What do you think is the best thing to do?" "What is your heart telling you?" "What do you hear God saying to you?" Questions imply capability. We want her to believe that she's capable. Even if she doesn't have an answer, just the fact that you asked communicates that you believe she's capable. She is bigger than her worries. She's stronger than whatever problem is facing her right now. She's got to do the work. But you can offer support through empathy, questions, and a whole lot of encouragement along the way.

Introduction

Hey! My name is Sissy. I'm so glad to get to meet you—although I really wish we were meeting in person rather than just in the pages of this book. I have a feeling we'd like each other. But for now, we can do our best to imagine how things would go if we were meeting in person.

Let's start with a little backstory. Maybe you've been worrying some lately.

Maybe you've been worried about what your friends think of you and whether they notice when you say the things that you think sound kind of awkward sometimes (and whether they're just acting like they don't notice). And then you replay what you said and try to figure out from their reaction if it really was awkward and if they'll want to keep hanging out with you. Your mind keeps thinking about it, over and over and over.

Maybe just being with others makes you nervous. Adults are fine, but people your age are a different story. It's hard to know what to say or when to say it. It's even hard to know who to talk to in unstructured social times, like at lunch or youth group. So it becomes easier to hang back or stay away from those situations completely. The problem is that the more you pull back, the harder it is to step back in. The worry becomes so consuming that it's all you can think about when you're with people, so spending time around other people happens less and less often. People besides your family, that is. But the worry about missing out nags at you too.

Or maybe you threw up with the last round of the flu. Now every time you get a little sick—or your stomach feels the slightest bit weird—you can't stop thinking that you might throw up. You end up making yourself feel sick just from thinking so much about being sick.

Maybe you can't fall asleep at night because your brain won't stop looping through all the things you worry about.

Maybe you've worried ever since you were little, although the topics have changed. And you've wondered, after hearing other people in school talk about anxiety, if that might be what's going on with you. Maybe you feel pretty sure it is.

Maybe, when you worry, things don't feel quite right, but you've found a few things that help. Things like counting even numbers, tapping, washing your hands, or checking on things. Maybe you have something you do that makes you feel better at bedtime, even though that thing doesn't totally feel like it makes sense.

Maybe you worry about getting worried, and that if the thing that happened recently really was a panic attack, you could have one again at any moment.

Now let's imagine your mom or dad has noticed. They've noticed because you're spending more time in your room, or you're missing school because of headaches. Maybe you're not interested in doing things with friends as much as you used to be. Or maybe you brought it up to them and they said, "We think it's time to talk to someone."

Those words can sound kind of ominous. "Talking to someone" about the things that are going on deep inside of you, when you've never even met that person, can feel intimidating or awkward.

Or it might not. You might have friends in counseling and you've been curious if it would help you too. You might have wanted to bring the subject up with your parents but weren't sure how or whether they would think something was wrong with you.

That's where I come in.

Let me interrupt our imagining to say that there is NOTHING wrong with you. Nothing at all—unless the same thing is wrong with almost one out of every three kids in your grade.[1] You are totally normal. In fact, you're a lot better than normal. But we'll come back to that.

I got us off the track of our story. Your parents told you—or you decided—it was time to try counseling. Now you've gotten pulled out of math class to come to my office. You drive up to an adorable yellow house with a white picket fence.

"Is this really where we're going?"

"Yes," your parents say. "This is Daystar."

(Daystar is where I get to sit with girls like you and their families every day, and have for almost thirty years. I sound a lot older than I feel, by the way.)

You walk in the front door of Daystar to find a lobby that looks more like a Pottery Barn living room than an office. Not exactly what you were expecting from a counselor's office.

You're greeted by smiling faces and given a tour of the house. You're even offered popcorn in our kitchen. After a few minutes, I come down the stairs to meet you, followed by my little therapy assistant, Lucy, a black-and-white fluff ball of a Havanese puppy.

Then we'd go upstairs to my office. I'd sit across from you, Lucy would likely sit right next to you or crawl up in your lap, and we'd start talking.

Actually, I'd start by telling you that anything you

tell me is confidential and that I want Daystar to feel like a safe place for you. In reality, as much as a book can, I want you to feel this book is a safe place too.

- A place for you to learn more about not only what's going on inside of you, but who you are.
- A place for you to write about what you're feeling and learning.
- A place for you to discover more of who God has made you to be and the immense strength and courage He has placed inside you.

This book is called *Brave* because that's what I believe you are already, even though we haven't actually met. There are a few reasons I know you're brave, which we'll get to later. For now, just reading this introduction means you're brave—that you know worry is something you struggle with and you're ready to fight it. I absolutely trust that you can.

I have a feeling whoever bought this book for you believes the same thing. So even though we haven't met, consider me a part of your team. That really is what I do for a living. I have the profound privilege of cheering on some of the most amazing girls in the world—girls just like you. My dog, Lucy, and I both do. It's a pretty incredible job. Plus, who wouldn't want to take their dog to work?

I hope I've already earned a little bit of your trust and that you'll keep reading. I really do think you'll finish this book not only knowing practical ways to fight your worry and anxiety, but also having found more of you along the way—with all of the bravery, strength, and heart God has placed inside of you.

Rules for Reading

Okay, they're not really rules. I don't want you to shut this book immediately. They're more like guidelines or even just things to remember. So cross out "Rules for Reading." Literally—take your pen and cross that statement out right now.

A Few Things to Remember

1. There is no wrong answer. The goal is for you to discover more of you, remember? What you feel and think is important. So I want you to write it, or draw it, if you're more of a draw-er.

2. Don't worry about someone finding this book and reading it. Okay, your little sister might, so maybe you should hide it somewhere good. But that's why I wrote the note in the beginning to your parents, letting them know this book is for you—to process your emotions on your own. Don't worry about them finding the book and reading what you've written. It's so important that you write about or draw your feelings. At some point, I'm also going to encourage you to talk about them.

3. Be honest with yourself. It's going to be hard to admit some of the things we talk about. It's hard sometimes to talk about struggles. It's especially hard when you want to do things right, which I imagine is true about you. It's true about me too, which is why I know. This book will only help, however, if you're honest.

4. Practice. This is actually the most important guideline. The number one reason girls—and really anyone—don't work through their anxiety is that they don't practice the skills they learn to fight the anxiety. So as we go through this book, I'm going to give you different types of homework. I know—not a fun word—but this homework will be fun. Actually, what's fun is the confidence I KNOW you will gain, although the work might be hard at times.

5. Share. I guess in number 3 I made it seem like you could just write or draw about things, but I really do want you to talk. I want you to know you're not alone in what you're feeling, which is why I'm including the stories of other girls in these pages. But I also want you to be talking to people you can see in-person, people who will be able to respond to you in real time. I want you to have other people on this team who are cheering you on—just like I am.

Here we go. . . .

Section One

Understanding

1. Defining the Worry Words

I don't think it's ever been harder to be a teenager than it is today. Especially a teenage girl. Again, I've been counseling girls for almost thirty years. That's a lot of years. And a lot of girls.

I'll share reasons why I believe the teen years are hard, but first, I'd love to know what you think. *Do you agree? Why do you think it's especially hard to be a teenage girl today?*

_____

_____

_____

_____

_____

_____

That's a great list, I'm sure. Here's something I want you to know as we go through this book together. What you're saying makes sense. I know, I know—I can't hear you. But I still know it's true. The most important thing is not even what you say, but that you're saying it. For that reason, there is going to be a lot of space in this book for you to journal—and draw too, if you're more of a draw-er than a journaler. I'd love for you to do a little of both.

Worry's Best Tricks

Anxiety has a lot of tricks it tries to play on you. We'll talk about specific tricks and tools in the "Help" section, but I'm going to go ahead and tell you two of worry's biggest tricks.

Worry tries to make you think

1) **something is wrong with you.**
2) **you're the only one who feels this way.**

Anxiety—we'll give him a better name later—is a big fat liar. Both statements above are untrue. Sadly, though, almost every girl I've met has believed those two things. It's why I want to disprove them both right here in the beginning. They're his best tricks, and he's the *worst* for trying to tell you those things.

Nothing is wrong with you. We're going to talk in chapter 2 about why you specifically might struggle with worry and anxiety, but I'll go ahead and tell you that rather than something being wrong with your brain, it means something is really right. And you're in good company. Actually, almost one in three kids struggle with anxiety,[1] and girls are twice as likely as boys.[2]

That means there's a good chance it's also happening to the girl who sits beside you in class, or the one whose locker is next to yours, or even the girl in your grade who intimidates you the most. It might be happening to your best friend too, and you don't know because neither of you has said it out loud. That's what happens with worry and anxiety. We have these thoughts . . . these scary thoughts that feel like they consume us at times. We feel like we're the only ones, so we don't say anything to anyone. The thoughts make us feel like something is wrong with us. Again, I can promise you that it's not. And we've already started to disprove the second idea; you can tell from the statistics that you're not alone. I sit with girls every day who have those kinds of thoughts looping around in their very normal, very smart brains. More on that later too.

You're not alone. C. S. Lewis wrote, "Friendship is born at that moment when one person says to another: What! You, too? I thought that no one but myself . . ."[3] Anxiety tries to make you feel like you are the only one who's ever worried this much or who has ever worried about something that sounds this silly. (It's really not silly, no matter what it is. It might sound silly to you when the worry passes, but it sure feels real when you're in the worry.)

Anxiety is an isolator. Because it makes us feel like something is wrong with us, we don't end up talking about it.

We've established that anxiety is a liar and an isolator. It's also very confusing, which is one reason it's particularly hard to be a teenage girl today.

I remember sitting with a group of girls your age not too long ago. We were talking about how common it is for teenage girls to use the word *anxiety* when describing themselves or how they felt about a certain situation. "I have anxiety," or "I had an anxiety attack last night," or "Such-and-such gives me anxiety." You know. You've heard these statements too. I will never forget the words one girl said: "We probably use the word so much because no one would listen if you just said you were stressed." All of the other girls agreed. *Have you ever felt that way?*

☐ For sure   ☐ No, not really

When I was growing up, if we wanted to really upset our parents, we might say, "I'm going to run away!" Now girls as young as eight are threatening to take their own lives when they're mad at their parents. I would imagine that you hear people talk about how "depressed they are," mention that they had a "panic attack" the night before, or throw around words like *suicidal* and *bipolar* and *PTSD* at the lunch table almost daily. Now, don't get me wrong—some of those girls might really be experiencing those struggles. But here's the problem: Some aren't. You know that already. Some just want big words to describe their big feelings. Others want someone to listen and feel like no one is, including their parents or their peers, so they think the bigger their words, the more likely someone will be to listen.

Here's another problem: When girls use those words when they're not really experiencing those things, the words lose their meaning. Then, when you're struggling, it's hard to know what the word really does mean or whether anyone will listen to you, because it feels like everyone your age today has anxiety.

That's where we're going to start, with the definitions of the words you hear thrown around a lot among girls your age. You might have even noticed that I've been using the words *worry* and *anxiety* interchangeably. Fear, worry, anxiety, stress, pressure, and even anxiety disorders are all important to understand in today's world. I truly believe that the more we know about worry and anxiety, the easier they are to beat. So let's start with a few definitions of these worry words, from a counselor's perspective.

The Worry Continuum

In the book for your parents, I talked about what I call "the worry continuum." It looks a little like this:

STRESS

hangs around
goes away   a little longer   loop-the-loop
                                       all day long

fear   worry   anxiety
of something   about something

Fear

It all starts with fear. Fears are those things we're afraid of . . . that maybe make us jump or even scream sometimes. You might be afraid of spiders, snakes, or jellyfish in the ocean. Those are three of my biggies. An important word with fear is that we're afraid *of* something. Fears are objects that our amygdala has developed an unpleasant emotional attachment to. We'll talk more about the amygdala later. But fear is usually attached to something, or even the threat of that thing. When the thing or the threat comes, our emotions take over. (According to my babysitter, Lauren, I'd only let her pick me up if there was a bug near me—or I thought there was. I'd scream, cry, and run to her.) When we are in the presence of the object we fear, we have a great deal of emotion, but once it's gone, so is the emotion. We move on.

What are your top three fears?

Worry

Fear changes to worry when it hangs around a little more. Worry is more pervasive, meaning it doesn't go away just because

27

we get away from the bug. We're not worried *of* something, we're worried *about* it. It revolves around more of a general subject than a specific object. We worry that someone we love might get cancer. We worry we won't make good enough grades or won't be able to beat our personal record in a track meet. We worry our friends are mad at us, or that we come off as awkward sometimes with other people.

What are three things you worry about?

Anxiety

Then there's anxiety. The word *anxiety* really has replaced the word *worry* for most girls your age I know, but anxiety is different from fear or worry. Anxiety can be about any of the things we feel afraid of or worried about—but instead of the fear or worry passing through our minds, it gets stuck. I tell girls all the time in my counseling office that it's like the one-loop roller coaster at the fair. You know it, if you've seen one. It's a roller coaster, but it doesn't go anywhere but the same loop, over and over and over. When you have anxiety, your scary thought circles around and around, and you just can't seem to make it stop.

If you had to say right now the thing that loops around the most in your brain—that you worry about and can't seem to make stop—what would it be? It can be something that makes a lot of sense, or even feels silly. *I've talked to girls who have looping thoughts about everything you can imagine. What's yours?*

You might even have a couple of things that loop in your brain. It could be that you had one thing a few years ago, but now you have a new thing that's replaced it. Maybe, when you were younger, you worried that something terrible would happen to your mom or dad. You could hardly stand to have a babysitter or for them to go out of town, you'd get so worried. Now maybe you worry about getting a bad grade or doing something wrong. Maybe you even feel like you have to tell your parents every single thing you ever do wrong, or even things you think you might do wrong. Maybe you got sick and threw up a few months ago, and now every time your tummy feels a bit off, you worry you're going to throw up again. Maybe you worry your friends don't want to be your friends any longer. That they think you're annoying and they're only being nice because they don't want to seem rude.

Naming the Worry

Here's the thing about anxiety. It's a little like the Whac-A-Mole game at Chuck E. Cheese. You remember—you are standing over a board, holding a hammer. A little mole pops up. And just when you bang the hammer down, he pops up somewhere else. And again.

And again. The mole knows how to get under your skin. Anxiety is the same. It's not only a liar and an isolator, but it's smart. In fact, I think it's time to interrupt this information on anxiety to go ahead and give him a name. It could be a him or her. It could even be an it. But my guess is that you already know his voice. He's the one who tells you things like these:

"You can't."

"It's too hard."

"You'll never do enough."

"The worst thing you can imagine happening is the thing that most likely will happen."

"You'll fail."

"They'll laugh."

"Your mom is going to get cancer."

"If you don't check and recheck the door, someone might come in and hurt your family."

"Someone already has come in and hurt your family, and they're on the way up the stairs to you."

That last sentence is something that used to loop in my brain when I was in high school. I'd lie awake in bed at night, terrified. I would imagine that someone had already killed my parents and was coming up the stairs to get me. I had this strange game I played with myself where I'd watch the clock and think, *If I just make it to 3:20, I'll be okay.* And *Now I have to make it to 3:30. Then I'll be okay.* And so on. Not only was the worry telling me the worst-case scenario had come true, but it was also telling me something I had to do to make myself feel better. I'd lie there in my bed, watching the clock, listening and obeying everything that worry told me. Only I didn't have anyone telling me that the voice wasn't true, that it was worry lying. And I certainly didn't know anyone else had ever felt the same way. I wish I had. I wish I had known that I could beat him. I think it would have helped me learn how to fight anxiety much younger than I did. Now I know how to recognize his voice and know not to give him any power. He doesn't deserve it. Not in my world or in yours.

What are some things worry says to you?

....

....

....

....

....

....

....

Let's come up with a name for that lying, isolating, smart, truly annoying voice that whispers those kinds of lies to you. We want to give him a name because I want you to remember that his voice is not yours. It's not yours, and it's not true. Many of the younger girls I work with call him the Worry Monster. One calls him Bob. I know some high school girls who call him things like the Great Exaggerator or He Who Must Not Be Named or just plain Worry, and I know one girl who named hers Agnes. The point is, we want to separate his (or her) voice from yours. Plus, it's easier to talk about him when he has a name.

As a side note, when we talk about someone who isolates and lies and is smart, it sure reminds me of someone else that you may be thinking of too. I did a podcast not too long ago with my friend Annie F. Downs. I don't know if you've read her books, but I highly recommend them. When we were talking about the Worry Monster, she looked at me and said, "Is it demonic?" I laughed and thought she was kidding, mostly because that's not a word I use to describe things very much. She wasn't kidding—and yes, it is, although calling it demonic might not be the way you normally talk about things either. Basically, she was saying, "Is that Satan's voice disguised as the Worry Monster?" It sure is. Satan, in Scripture, is called the Father of Lies. John 8:44 says, "He was a murderer from the beginning, not holding to the truth, for there is no truth in him. When he lies, he speaks his native language, for he is a liar and the father of lies." I absolutely believe that his voice and the worry voice you hear in your head are one and the same. Call him the Enemy if you'd rather—but only if thinking of him that way won't cause you more anxiety. I don't want you to have a looping thought that Satan is in your head. He's not. He just tries to lie and trick you into worrying, just like he tries to trick you into other destructive things. The great news is that Jesus has already beaten him and given you the power to beat him too—whatever name you call him.

Because of how smart and sneaky he is, I'm going to call him the Worry Whisperer for now. Regardless of what we call him, we need to understand his ways. The more we learn about him, the easier it is to fight him.

Here's what we've learned about the Worry Whisperer so far:

- He's a liar.
- He's an isolator.
- He's confusing.
- And he's smart, in a sneaky kind of way.

The Whac-a-Mole Ways of Worry

The Worry Whisperer knows the things that you are most likely to worry about at any given age. He knows the thing that would be the scariest in second grade—like something bad happening to your parents. And sixth grade—like throwing up. And tenth grade—like failing a certain subject or being abandoned by friends. He then takes those intrusive thoughts (intrusive because they intrude on whatever you're thinking about right then) and drops them into your brain. Because those thoughts represent the scariest thing you can imagine at that particular age, they are the thoughts that have the most power. Therefore, they're the thoughts that get stuck. Whac-a-mole. You beat him in one area in second grade. He pops up in a different way in sixth. And so on. The great news is the tools that beat him in second grade work in sixth and tenth as well. They continue to work when you're a grown-up too. Anxiety expert Tamar Chansky says that although "anxiety is the number one mental health problem facing children and adolescents today . . . it is also the most treatable."[4] We're gonna prove together just how weak this Worry Whisperer is!

I do want to mention two more words that aren't used much in your world anymore, though they certainly should be. *Stress* and *pressure*. We're going to talk about them both in the next chapter. Stress is a powerful force and one that kicks the Worry Whisperer into high gear. I believe you live with profoundly more stress than I did when I was growing up, and more than your mom and grandmother grew up with. You live with more pressure to get things right, to succeed, to look beautiful, and to have all of your friends and followers on social media respond. It's a lot.

I'm going to use the words *worry* and *anxiety* in this book interchangeably, mostly because some of you live more in the land of worry, some of you struggle more with anxiety, and some of you flip back and forth. In fact, we all worry at least a little—people who don't worry at all certainly aren't reading this book.

When to Worry about Your Level of Worry

Actually, I don't ever want you to worry about your worry. Maybe we should call this section "When to Make Sure You Have Someone in Your Life to Help You with Your Level of Worry." In this book, we're going to be talking about worry and anxiety both. I do want you to know that we can feel anxious and even struggle with anxiety without it being "diagnosable." Diagnosable anxiety is what the folks in my profession would refer to as a disorder. It could also be called clinical anxiety at that point. Clinical anxiety comes in many shapes and sizes. There's social anxiety, phobias (debilitating fears around certain objects), panic disorder, and panic attacks. Obsessive-compulsive disorder and post-traumatic stress disorder (PTSD) are very similar to anxiety disorders. And then there's the wider diagnosis of generalized anxiety disorder, as well as several others. Just because you identify with the anxiety we talk about in this book does not necessarily mean that you have one of these or any kind of anxiety disorder. Don't jump to diagnosing yourself. Your feelings are valid even without a diagnosis. You don't want to be defined by a struggle you're experiencing.

If any of the following apply to you, I want you to talk to someone. Show your parents this section of the book and let them know I said it was time.

- If your anxiety is debilitating, meaning you aren't able to do or think about anything else when the anxiety hits.
- If it interrupts your daily life.
- If you try the things in this book and they don't seem to help—or they don't help enough.
- If anxiety is affecting at least two of the three most important parts of your life: your family, your friends, your schoolwork.
- If it's gone on for at least six months.

Anxiety left untreated only gets worse. It can also lead to depression when it goes on for too long. But we're not going to let it.

Here's the good news: You can do this. You're not alone. You've got me, and you've got people in your life who love you and want to help. You've got a God who delights in you and has beaten every Worry Whisperer that's ever been or ever will be. And I know that you've got more strength, more resourcefulness, more grit, and more brave going on inside of you than you think. God made you that way. I can't wait for you to see that version of you in action.

What are three things you've learned so far?

_____

_____

_____

_____

_____

_____

I want you to write a letter here to the Worry Whisperer.
What would you want to say to him?

_____

_____

_____

_____

_____

_____

_____

_____

_____

_____

_____

_____

_____

_____

A Few *Brave* Things to Remember

- It's never been harder to be a teenage girl than it is today.

- Worry tries to make you think something is wrong with you and you're the only one who feels this way. Neither is true.

- Anxiety is a liar and an isolator. It's also very confusing.

- *Fears* have to do with something we're afraid of—that our amygdala has developed an unpleasant emotional attachment to. *Worry* doesn't go away just because we get away from the thing we're afraid of. It's more about a general subject than a specific object. *Anxiety* is when those fears are worries that get stuck—much like the one-loop roller coaster at the fair.

- It's important to give your anxiety a name so you can remember that his voice is not only not yours, but it's also not true.

- The subject your worry loops around changes as you get older. Basically, it's the scariest thing you can imagine happening at any specific age.

- Anxiety left untreated only gets worse. If your worry or anxiety seems to be getting worse, or you're just not sure what to do to make it better, talk to your mom or dad. Find a grown-up at school or church you can trust and who can help you find your way to help—and to beating this lying, isolating, confusing Worry Whisperer. You can do this!

2. Why Me?

I want to know what you think. *What do you believe are the reasons why you worry?* I don't mean the things you worry about, but why you struggle with worry or anxiety.

_____

_____

_____

_____

_____

_____

_____

I wish I could see your list. If I had to guess, I would imagine that you wrote a few phrases like "I'm too _____" or "I'm not _____ enough."

"I care too much about what people think."

"I overthink things too much."

"I'm too sensitive."

"I'm not independent enough."

"I'm not confident enough."

"I'm not brave enough."

Maybe you should go back and add to that list now. What are really the reasons you suspect that you worry?

Years ago I read something I'll never forget. You know how we have those things? It's because I realized when I read it how true it was. It said that when something goes wrong in a boy's world, he blames someone else. When something goes wrong in a girl's world, she blames herself. RIGHT?! It's why I'd guess your list had several negative things on it that you believe are true about you.

The other reason I know those sentences are on your list is that I have heard thousands of girls say them over the years. I would guess you say something like them every single day. I would also guess that you get angry with yourself far more often than you get angry with anyone else. I know those sentences because I get it—I do the same. I think one of the Worry Whisperer's other worst tricks is that he tries to get us to blame ourselves for things that are either out of our control or aren't blameworthy to begin with.

I want to set the record straight here, not just about why you worry, but about you. Those sentences simply aren't true. Now, maybe you are sensitive. Perhaps you don't have a lot of confidence or you don't feel like you're very brave. But any time you use the words *too much* or *not enough*, that's when you know you're believing the Father of Lies again. We all have areas where we struggle. I often think of it like muscles. My math muscle isn't great—and neither is my patience muscle. Those are muscles I continue to work on as an adult. (Okay, truth be told, I don't really work on my math muscle much anymore.) Even if there is a little truth to those statements, those are EXACTLY the muscles we're going to be building together in this book! You're not too much or not enough anything. For now, let's talk about why you really worry. And then we'll come back to the truth of who you are.

The Externals

A few times in this book I'm going to have to tell you to trust me. This is one of them. The overwhelming majority of the reasons you struggle with worry and anxiety don't have anything to do with who you are on the inside. They're externals. They're parts of your life that you didn't choose or that you didn't have any control over. They're outside of you. External—get it? Remember, I've been counseling for almost thirty years. And I forgot to say, when I wrote the book for your parents, I read twenty-three books on the topic of anxiety. I really do know a lot about the subject. Let's talk about some of those externals I've learned about through counseling and research.

The Family Trickle-Down

Who in your family are you most like?

How are the two of you similar?

I wonder if part of how you're similar is that you both struggle with worry. There's a great chance it's your mom that you're most like in the worry category, but it could be your dad. It could even be a grandparent or an aunt. Now, your worry might look different than theirs, but you still have a worry trickle-down that affects you. In fact, if you have a parent who has anxiety, you're up to seven times more likely to experience it yourself.[1] And your family member might not even understand that the name for what's happening is anxiety.

My mom died this past year. I still miss her so much. She loved my sister and me like crazy. And remember, the things that are most important to us are the things that can easily start to loop. My sister and I were what our mom worried about the most. She would often say, "Worrying is a mother's job." She also often said that she did NOT have anxiety. My sister and I knew the truth . . . and I would guess that now in heaven she does too. She had anxiety, especially when it came to my sister and me.

When I turned sixteen, I got a car. I know, I was really lucky. It was a cool car—an old navy blue BMW with a sunroof and a tape deck, which was how we played music in our cars before Bluetooth. It also came with a twenty-four-inch rusted metal spike, courtesy of my mom. She told me it was for me to use to shatter my window if I went off a bridge so I could swim out. Yep. I'm serious. If she were sitting here, she would tell you it was very important that I keep it in my car at all times. My sister and I also got pepper spray in our stockings every single year. I guess our version of Santa had a little anxiety too.

For both of us, it trickled down. However, my sister's and my worries look really different. Let me also insert here that if you're the oldest, it's very likely to trickle down to you first. It definitely hits the younger sister (and brother) sometimes too, but the oldest almost always catches some of it. My sister, Kathleen, and I are sixteen years apart. Yes, you read that right. I was SHOCKED when my parents told me they were pregnant. Because we're so far apart in age, it's a little like we're both the oldest—or only children—in our birth order, and we both caught some of the anxiety.

My anxiety comes more in the form of a type A personality. I'm a perfectionist. If you've ever studied the Enneagram, I'm a 1. (If you haven't, check out *The Road Back to You* book or podcast. It's my favorite personality study out there.) The fact that I'm a 1 means I don't necessarily feel anxious on a daily basis, but I am highly productive. I get so much done, and quickly. I was always the first to finish a test in school. My room was clean. My bed was made. And still, when I find myself putting everything back in order in my house, I realize that I'm worried about something. It's all about order for me. Order might be the thing that helps you feel better too. If so, you hate it when your brother comes in and messes up your room. Sometimes you have to line things up just so, or put your clothes out the night before, or do all kinds of organized or efficient things to help yourself feel better.

Kathleen is different. She's organized, but she doesn't have to be, which is awesome for her. She might even say that my need to be organized drives her a little crazy. (She probably wouldn't say that out loud, because she's super sweet. You'd really like her.) She's an Enneagram 6 and has a primary need for security. Having someone listen and worry with her really helps her. She also, however, doesn't seem worried. She says she's like a duck gliding on the water, looking very smooth and unruffled but paddling her feet as fast and furiously as she can underneath the surface.

We both caught the trickle-down. You might have too. Your anxiety might look different from your mom's or dad's, but it's still there. You hear theirs in how often they ask you where you'll be going or what time you'll be home. You likely know just what your worried family member's Worry Whisperer sounds like. And there's a significant chance their Worry Whisperer tries to make them worry about you.

Here's the thing. You can't call them out on their anxiety. If you were to tell them those things aren't important or are just their Worry Whisperer talking, it might not go over so well. They would likely use the word *disrespect*, and you might end up grounded. We sure wouldn't want that. But what you can do is remind each other. You can ask your mom or dad to get a copy of *Raising Worry-Free Girls*. Many parents I've talked to started reading that book for their daughters and found themselves in the pages. You can ask them to read this book after you do. Then you can gently remind each other when you hear the Worry Whisperer coming through. You can tell them, "Your Worry Whisperer is getting my Worry Whisperer stirred up," as long as you say it respectfully. I have a nine-year-old friend who tells her mom sometimes, "It sounds like the Worry Monster is talking to you again, Mom." She says it with respect, which means it goes over much better.

You want your mom or dad to help you with this fight against the Worry Whisperer, but you can help them too. There's a whole lot more strength when you're fighting together than when you're each fighting on your own. And that strength and resilience are two of your most important tools in this fight, regardless of your external situation.

From Trouble to Trauma

Just like with the words *anxiety* and *depression*, I'm sure you're hearing the word *trauma* a lot too. I certainly am. It's another one of those words we seem to be using more in the past few years. We use it to describe all manner of things, including horrific events— such as watching someone die—and even as a type of slang. You might have experienced talking to a friend about something you struggle with when someone else overheard you and said, with more sarcasm than concern, "Trauma."

What does trauma really mean? Let me give you the clinical definition first. According to the American Psychological Association, "A traumatic event is one that threatens injury, death, or the physical integrity of self or others and also causes horror, terror, or helplessness at the time it occurs. Traumatic events include sexual abuse, physical abuse, domestic violence, community and school violence, medical trauma, motor vehicle accidents, acts of terrorism, war experiences, natural and human-made disasters, suicides, and other traumatic losses." The article goes on to say that more than two-thirds of us have experienced a traumatic event by the age of sixteen.[2]

Here's some good news: *Trauma* is really a newer word we have for trouble that has been around for a long time. John 16:33 is a verse we're going to talk more about in the last section of the book: "In this world you will have trouble. But take heart! I have overcome the world." It could also read, "In this world you will have trauma." The rest of that verse is what enables us to go through trauma. We do not go through it alone. Jesus has overcome the world, and He eventually redeems every bit of trauma that we experience. You will likely go through trauma and be even stronger and more resilient for having gone through it. It's what research says,[3] and it's certainly the case for many girls I know.

Take Ellen. She was young when her parents divorced. Several years later, her dad remarried a woman that Ellen was close to. One weekend, when Ellen and her brother were staying with their dad, an argument erupted in their house. The argument escalated and got physical. Ellen heard the yelling and ushered her brother into another room where he wouldn't have to see what was happening. Her stepmom called the police, and Ellen watched her dad get in the back of a police car and be driven away. It was traumatic for Ellen.

Take Lily. When Lily was ten, she lost her mom. It was completely unexpected. Her family was at home. She was the first one to call 9-1-1 after her mom's stroke. She witnessed not only what happened, but the aftermath of her dad's panic and devastation. All of it was what we would consider trauma.

Take Katherine. Katherine's dad was a drug addict. When he was sober, she would get to see him. When he wasn't, her mom would make sure she wasn't exposed to the dangerous situations that arose from his behavior while he was on drugs. But it was hard to know when he was using and when he wasn't . . . and hard to anticipate the risky situations he might put Katherine in. Not only did he put her in traumatic situations over the years, but their relationship itself was traumatic for Katherine.

Take Hannah. Hannah was bullied over and over by a group of girls when she was in elementary school. One afternoon, one of the girls grabbed her on the playground, pushed her to the ground, and proceeded to kick her as the other girls stood around laughing. That traumatic scene has been etched into Hannah's mind.

I could tell you stories of literally thousands of girls like Katherine, Lily, Ellen, and Hannah. They are four strong, resourceful, courageous young women whom I admire greatly. I have watched God at work in redeeming their stories through the strength of these girls. It's not complete. It's still hard. But I wish I'd had more of their courage when I was in high school. I wish I'd had more of yours.

You've been through hard things too. Let me say that differently. You've *survived* hard things. You came through. Some of the hard things have been trauma, and some have been milder forms of trouble. You might not have felt strengthened by it in the middle of it. You may have experienced sadness and anger. You may have had trouble sleeping. You may have had trouble concentrating in school. You may have had more frequent stomachaches or headaches. I would imagine you did have more worry and anxiety. That's part of why we're talking about trauma in this section of the book. When trouble and trauma come, those of us who worry and get anxious become more worried and anxious. In fact, for two-thirds of you reading this book, it's why you became worried and anxious to begin with. But still, you persisted. You hung on. You're here and reading now.

Let me go ahead and say that you may feel like you haven't persisted. You feel grateful for the word *trauma*, because it feels like it legitimizes what you've been through and still feel like you're going through to some degree.

Trauma impacts all of us differently. We can and often do experience more resilience and strength in the aftermath. For some, though, that resilience takes a little longer. For those individuals, the trauma continues to impact them over and over. Rather than just the worry loop, for them, it's a specific scene or memory that plays repeatedly in their minds. Here's what happens, from a psychological standpoint. Our brains typically store memories in our long-term memory. You can recall them randomly or with intention, like when you hear a song from your childhood or you talk with your mom and dad about a trip you went on when you were little. You remember, but those memories come and go with normalcy. Traumatic memories, however, sometimes don't make it to long-term memory. They get stuck in the short-term. It's why when I counsel someone who has watched a family member die or who has been sexually abused, the memory can tend to replay itself over and over in their mind. They're not trying to remember. They just do—and at really random times. If this is happening to you, tell your mom or dad. Tell your school counselor or a grown-up you trust who can help. There are specific types of counseling that can help you talk about the trauma in a way that stores that memory where it's supposed to go so you don't have to relive it over and over.

Regardless of whether you are living in the resilience phase now or not quite yet, it is important to know that our experiences impact our anxiety. When you're struggling in another area, your worry and anxiety will often be worse. Mine sure is. We want to pay attention to when and why our worry and anxiety increase. We want to write and talk about those experiences and the worries that come. We also want to look for the ways God is redeeming them.

Write about a memory that's traumatic for you or one that felt like trouble. How have you seen God in it? How are you stronger for having gone through it? If it doesn't feel like you're stronger yet, what do you think He's saying to you in the middle of it?

The Trouble with Technology

Okay—don't be mad at me. I'm sure your parents have said a lot of this. You might have even read some of the articles. Just hear me out for a minute.

Yes, technology use has been connected to higher rates of anxiety and depression among teenagers. There has been an overall decline in the mental well-being of teenagers since smartphones became popular.[4] (I know. Now I sound like your grandmother.)

One article I read said that people your age who spend five to seven hours per day on their smartphones "are twice as likely to report being depressed as those who use their phones for one to two hours a day."[5] Yes, I know that's depression and we're talking about anxiety, but the two often go hand in hand. And I honestly don't want you to have to struggle with either.

Another article (one of many) named several ways technology use contributes to anxiety: social comparison, lack of an ability to regulate emotions, increased social anxiety from avoiding social interaction, fear of not being connected enough, and cyberbullying, which studies show can lead to anxiety, depression, and suicidal thoughts.[6]

I do know there are positives that come from technology use as well. Zoom and FaceTime certainly keep us connected when we can't be together in person. Technology also gives us opportunities to learn many different skills, even social and emotional skills such as empathy and mindfulness. But I also want to tell you what I hear directly from girls. These are the top five ways I see technology impact the lives of girls your age:

1. Interacting primarily on screens creates a false sense of security. The anxiety that can come with the awkwardness of in-person interaction is removed. I know . . . it sounds like a good thing. And it would be if we were living in the world of *WALL-E* and you could stay on your screen constantly, but you have to go out into the real world. You have to learn how to connect in real time. I'm going to say

46

it over and over, but to work through your anxiety, you have to do the thing that makes you afraid.

2. Interacting primarily on screens also creates a false sense of relationship. You know this, but you can't really read someone else's face as well as you can in person, even if you're on FaceTime. The same sentence in a text could be kind or sarcastic. Someone can act like your best friend after having just started following you on social media. It happens to grown-ups too. Relationships develop slowly, over time. Technology speeds things up and skips over some of the important parts of building not only relationships, but trust. It's easy to end up trusting others who haven't quite earned it, or who aren't who they say they are.

3. Social media, in particular, feeds the comparison monster, and we all know comparison is the thief of joy. Everyone else looks like they have closer friends, are invited to more parties, get along better with their siblings. Just think about the fact that so many people remove posts if they don't get enough likes. That's basically saying your experience isn't important or valid unless enough people approve. And I, for example, truly like so many things a day and don't remember to click the button saying that I virtually like the post. Likes are not an accurate reflection of how another feels about us, and we certainly don't want others to have the power to validate us or our experiences.

4. Technology use increases your brain activity to a degree that is similar to actual anxiety. I talked to a psychiatrist several years ago who told me that when we're being bombarded by images on a screen, our brains move into a heightened state of agitation. Because your brain isn't finished developing, it's harder for it to calm back down. Therefore, too much stimulation on screens can make you more anxious, just from what you're taking in visually.

5. The pressure to keep up is constant and overwhelming. Let's just take Snapchat streaks, if those are still a thing by the time you read this (because we know how quickly things change in the world of technology). How many streaks do you have going? How long have they lasted? How much time a day does it take you to respond not just to your streaks, but to all the other communication via technology? I have talked to countless girls over the years who've disabled Snapchat for this very reason. It was just too much. I also know more and more girls who are taking breaks from technology in general for the same reasons. I know one amazing high school girl who decided to trade her smartphone in for a flip phone. They can't keep up. The fear that they'll hurt someone's feelings or communicate something unintended by not responding on all of the different platforms is too much pressure when they're already feeling plenty of pressure otherwise.

What about you? What would you add to the list of how technology increases anxiety?

_____

_____

_____

_____

How would you say technology negatively affects your life?

_____

_____

_____

_____

_____

What about the positives? How does it help?

_____

_____

_____

_____

_____

Do the positives or the negatives seem more significant?

_____

_____

How could you pull back a little on your technology use?

_____

_____

_____

_____

_____

What would you say to an eleven-year-old who is just start-ing her journey with technology and social media?

_____

_____

_____

_____

_____

The Power of Pressure

Let's talk about pressure. It may be last on this list of external factors that contribute to anxiety, but I believe it might be the most significant in this day and time.

I want you to create a pie chart for how you spend your time. I know, a pie chart might sound kind of goofy, but humor me. I want you to list homework, your school day, any sports activities you participate in, music lessons, leadership activities, all the things you do regularly with your time. Maybe list screens too, for kicks.

Now I want you to include creative time, rest time (not sleeping), _____ time (insert your name, which means time when you get to do whatever you want).

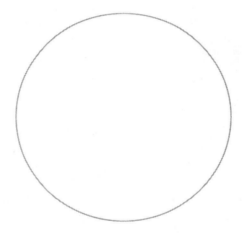

It was really interesting to counsel girls at the beginning of the COVID-19 pandemic. Many of the girls I saw I had already been seeing because of anxiety. When we first started hearing about the pandemic, I saw the anxiety get worse in more than a few of those girls. There were a lot of unknowns. Would their grandparents get sick? Would *they* get it? Were schools going to stay open? Were we going to go into lockdown? It was unpredictable and unknown, which are two things that worry hates.

A few weeks later, we were at home, because the state government had asked most people to stay home to limit the spread of the virus. The virus was surging, but folks were taking great care to stay safe. Classes were happening online. And girls under the age of eleven were hopping onto their video counseling calls with me with stuffed animals in hand, much more joyful and free than I had seen them since they started coming to counseling in the first place. The things that were making them anxious—friendships, school pressure, the pressure to perform—all those things were gone. They were having a blast baking with their moms and walking their dogs with their dads.

Girls your age weren't super different. I have several groups of high school girls I meet with in group counseling sessions. From them, I heard words like *bored* and *lonely*. But there seemed to be a collective sigh that was a long time coming. I asked those girls what, from the time at home, they would want to carry forward into post-pandemic time. They said things like "Playing games with my family," "Going for walks in the neighborhood," "Playing outside," "Family dinners," "Having time to think." One girl said, "I never knew I liked to be by myself. And I really do!"

A girl in one of the groups is a classic overcommitter. She runs track, is involved in student government, acts in plays, volunteers for an organization that benefits kids who have cancer . . . oh, and makes straight As. She also comes to the weekly group counseling meeting, but she misses often, or is late, or has to leave early because her activities overlap. She is *always* stressed.

Does that sound familiar at all?

When I asked the group what they wanted life to be like post-pandemic, she said, "I hope I remember what this time has been like. I want to make sure I'm not doing as much as I have in the past few years. It was just too much, and I feel like I'm discovering more of who I am with this extra time."

Up until that point, the girls in her group would suggest the same thing every week. "Why don't you stop doing just one thing?" they'd ask. Her response was always, "I just can't. I don't know what I'd drop." She lived in this state of perpetual low-grade anxiety, and she'd do fine for months and then crash. It took its toll.

Does *that* sound familiar at all?

I remember another girl who told me that she wouldn't stop any of her activities, even though she knew it was too much and they made her anxious. "Anxiety is what keeps me going," she said. She would run on that anxiety for weeks at a time and then hit a very emotional, very loud, angry, and yelling-at-her-mom kind of wall.

It's too much. When you look at your pie chart, do you have that feeling? Can you relate to either of these girls? If you struggle with worry and anxiety, I really would love for you to think long and hard—and pray and talk to your parents—about what you might give up.

Write at least one thing you feel like you could give up, if not a few.

_____

_____

_____

_____

What would make it hard to make that decision?

_____

_____

_____

_____

_____

_____

If the reasons you don't want to give something up involve pleasing others—not wanting to hurt the feelings of a teacher or coach or friend—I want you to trust me on this. Your mental health is more important. Your teacher or coach will eventually understand. Your friends will too. The truth is that you can give more out of a place of rest than a place of emptiness. You're not being selfish. You'll actually have more to offer in the long run. Think about it.

The Internals

The Gifts of Temperament

I have a feeling that last section was hard for you to read. That's because I do feel like I know you. I feel like I know you because (1) you care enough about working through worry to pick up this book, and (2) every single girl who struggles with worry and anxiety has a few things in common.

Those things in common have to do with what's referred to as temperament. Temperament is a little like your personality, although it runs deeper. According to a *Science Daily* article, *temperament* is defined as "biologically based individual differences in the way people emotionally and behaviorally respond to the world." The article goes on to state, "During infancy, temperament serves as the foundation of later personality."[7] In other words, temperament is who God made you to be from your earliest self. And here are a few things I know to be true about who you are:

- You're bright (which really means you're smart—in an inspired kind of way).
- You're conscientious (which means you want to get it right—whatever "it" is).
- You care deeply (for people and about how people see you).

- Things matter to you (you feel deeply in response to others).
- You try hard (at just about everything you do).

How many of those things are true about you? I really would guess every one of them. I would also guess that it's hard to admit those are true because you don't want to come off as bragging. Here's the thing: It's your temperament. It's who God made you to be. So when you admit how He's gifted you, He's the one who's getting the credit. Not you. You're safe to admit those things here.

Now that we've established how awesome you are, we can talk more about what that means. When I was little—way back in the 1970s—we didn't have iPhones. We didn't even have iPods. Actually, we didn't even have CDs or cassettes. We had records. You probably know about records, because they've become cool again. There were 33s, which were the equivalent of a whole album (they actually were albums, which is funny that we still call something an album that only comes through on your phone), and then there were 45s. Forty-fives were records that had one song on one side and another on the other. You bought the 45 for a single—a really popular song on the radio at the time. But the artist got you to listen to their other song because it was on the flip side. And it usually wasn't the best song on the album.

Those temperament kinds of gifts we listed before are a little like 45s. They are great on one side, but when you flip them over, they aren't necessarily so great. In fact, sometimes they cause us trouble. We could say that every one of our gifts, on the other side, is a curse. I don't really like that wording, though. Let's say it's your flip side. Let's go back to the gifts and look a little at the flip sides.

54

- You're bright, which means you don't miss things. You notice when one of your friends acts upset with you. You pick up on the fact that you were the last chosen for a team. You put two and two together and realize that you were the only girl from your group of friends not on the group text. Other girls might miss these things, but you don't. You're bright, which is great . . . and hard.

- You're conscientious, so you don't just want to get it right—you want to get all things right. You don't know when to let certain things go. You're not okay with just an A—you want a 100 or better. It's not that you're trying to beat others. You're trying to beat the standard you have for yourself, and that standard is exceedingly high.

- You care deeply. You work hard not to leave others out. You don't want anyone to feel like you were unkind, so you go back over and over things you've said to friends or acquaintances to make sure you didn't say something "wrong" or awkward or that might have hurt their feelings.

- Things matter to you. Other girls seem to let things roll off their backs, but everything tends to stop right in the middle of yours. Not only do you worry about what others think, but you can't stop thinking about it sometimes. When one of your friends is quiet, you don't realize that she might be having a bad day. You automatically jump to thinking she's mad at you.

- You try hard. You don't know when or how to stop trying. You try your very hardest for everything you attempt, no matter how small. Every single detail feels like it has to be taken care of, and in the right way . . . at least in public. Home is the one place where maybe you don't try all the way all the time, and then you just end up taking your frustrations out on your mom or little brother. It's not that you mean to, but it just seems to happen. Everywhere else, though, you're trying to be kind and get good grades and be a leader and inclusive and *so many things*. And then we circle right back around to pressure.

How many of those flip side kinds of things would you say are true about you? How do you see your flip side play out?

....

....

....

....

....

Your gifts and your flip side are the same thing. We couldn't take away the flip side without taking away the gifts. And your good gifts are part of who God made you to be. The way I think of it is that it's just hard to turn down the volume at times. Turning down the volume on the flip side helps you live more in the gifts. We're going to get there. That's so much of what this book is about. Your gifts are truly that—gifts. But anxiety takes those gifts and flips them over in a way that trips you up and gets you stuck. Just like that one-loop roller coaster at the fair. And there's one more kind of roller coaster that I want to mention.

The Roller Coaster of Development

I've noticed that when I tell younger girls the things outlined above about who they are—bright, conscientious, caring—huge smiles spread across their faces. I'll say, "Is that true?" And every one of them nods and says, "Yes!" For girls your age, however, it's different.

I tell someone your age the wonderful things I believe are true about who God made her to be, and the most I get in reply is an "I guess." I would guess that you would say the same thing. It's complicated. Yes, those things are true. But you know, as we just talked about, they also trip you up sometimes. Or you're not even sure you believe them anymore. Or one day you do and the next day you don't. Up and down. Up and down . . . just like a one-loop roller coaster.

More than 1,300 girls ages eight to eighteen were surveyed in a recent poll. They were asked to rate their confidence on a 0 to 10 scale. Between the ages of eight and fourteen, the confidence levels of girls dropped 30 percent, from 8.5 to 6.[8] That's a pretty significant drop.

Where would you rate your confidence level today?

What about when you were in elementary school?

Why do you think your confidence might have dropped?

What has changed about you?

_____

_____

_____

_____

_____

I would guess that nothing has changed about you, other than that you've gotten a little taller, you've gotten a lot smarter, and how you see yourself is different. I hope that poll reminds you of another very important truth: The changes are completely normal. You're not the only one whose confidence dropped with the beginnings of puberty.

I'd also love for you to stop reading right now and Google *Always #likeagirl*. It's an advertisement I show at parenting seminars all over the country to remind parents what it's like to be a girl your age. Can you relate? I've literally seen thousands of girls who experience that drop in confidence during puberty that the girls in the ad describe. I would imagine that you also feel less confident, less free to share your opinion, less sure of yourself in relationships, and a whole lot of other lesses too, in these post-puberty years. We're going to talk about that again in chapter 8, but here's something important for you to know: Those lesses are not any more true about you than the too muches and not enoughs we talked about at the beginning of the chapter. You are exactly who and where you're supposed to be.

The shifts in your perspective have to do with changes going on in your body and in your brain, which influence how you think. We'll talk more about your thinking later, but let's talk about what's happening in your body for now. There are some significant changes taking place as you enter puberty and even as your period is getting regulated. And, no, don't worry—I'm not going to talk a lot about your period and embarrass you. I'll only say that from a scientific perspective, it's not only known to affect your emotions, but how you feel about yourself too.[9] You know that. You experience it every month. But I want to talk to you about something you may not know.

When you were a little girl and learning to walk and talk and all of those important things, as you can imagine, your brain was growing really fast. Then, when you were in elementary school, it had a period where the growth slowed down. It's different for every girl, but as you moved closer to puberty and hormones started wreaking havoc on your brain, the growth started up again. It began growing so fast that it was like too much electricity running through the wiring of an old house. Have the lights ever flickered when you turned on your hair dryer? There is more electricity than the wiring can handle. Your brain, in these years, short-circuits. There is more growth than your brain can handle. When it short-circuits, it primarily affects two things: your memory and your confidence. The ironic thing is that we're going to talk about how anxiety ALSO affects your memory. Anxiety affects your confidence too. So you've got a double whammy from an anxiety and a developmental perspective. Both cause your confidence to dip, on top of some of the other ways your brain thinks in these years that we'll look at later. For now, though, let's just say you've got a lot of knocks against your confidence. You've got a lot of reasons NOT to see your gifts and to live in and dwell on the flip side of those very gifts. And I want us to flip that record right back over.

You are bright.

You are conscientious.

You care deeply.

Things matter to you.

You try hard.

I would also guess that you're really kind.

And I KNOW that you're brave.

The Worry Whisperer tries to make you think none of those things are true. The definition I came up with in the book for your parents is that anxiety is an overestimation of the problem and an underestimation of yourself.[10] The Worry Whisperer wants you to live in the too-much and not-enough and less places—the underestimation of yourself. If you live there, you won't fight him. You won't believe you can, and he can keep you right where he wants you . . . worried and defeated. I know that's not where you want to be. I know you want more. I know you want to be able to face the things that make you afraid. I know you want to have freedom from your worries. I know you want to experience the you that you know is somewhere deep inside and the gifts God has placed within your bright, brave self.

I want you to take a minute and do a little homework. I want you to make sure you keep the Worry Whisperer completely out of the room. We're not going to give his voice any power. And I want you to try really hard to listen to that voice inside of you—God's voice saying who you are.

Draw a circle. Inside that circle I want you to write ten ways that you believe God has gifted you—who He has made you to be. Don't worry about bragging. It's not a thing here. They're His gifts—remember, He's the one getting credit. *Now, out to the side of the circle, I want you to write down five to ten lies you believe that the Worry Whisperer tells you.*

This book is going to help you live more in the middle of that circle. That's what we're going for . . . living where his voice doesn't have the power to define you. And it doesn't. Only God does. So let's talk a little more about why and how this book can help you see and experience the gifted, bright, strong, brave young woman God uniquely made you to be.

A Few *Brave* Things to Remember

- One of Worry's worst tricks is that he tries to get us to blame ourselves for things that are either out of our control or that aren't blameworthy to begin with.

- Most of the reasons you struggle with worry are externals—they're in your family makeup, they're a result of something hard that's happened in your life, they're related to the pressure surrounding the lives of girls today, or they're even a result of the effects of screens on your brain.

- You've been through hard things—and God can use those very things to create more resilience and strength in you. Often the worry gets worse in the short-term, but God can and will redeem every hard thing you've been through. It's important to talk about those things with a trusted adult, especially if you're in the season when those things seem to be making the worry worse.

- Technology use has been connected to higher rates of anxiety and depression among teenagers, and these are five common ways it impacts our lives: it creates a false sense of security; it creates a false sense of relationship; it feeds the comparison monster; it actually creates anxiety-like brain activity; and it leads to an overwhelming pressure to keep up.

- All of the girls I've ever met who are anxious have a few things in common: they're bright and conscientious, they care and feel deeply, and they try hard. Those very gifts are sometimes the things that make us more anxious. It can be hard to turn down the volume knob on all of the caring and aware-ing.

- You're at an age when girls' confidence dips naturally—even the girls who look confident. It has to do with the way your brain is growing and your hormones are changing. It's completely normal, and those feelings you're having of not being enough are simply not true.

- Anxiety is an overestimation of the problem and an underestimation of yourself. Worry's voice does not have the power to define you. That job belongs to you and the God who loves and delights in you.

3. How Will This Help?

Think about a time when you got really anxious recently. *What was it about? How did you respond? How well did your response work?*

_____

_____

_____

_____

_____

_____

Spoiler alert: Most of our attempts to deal with worry and anxiety on our own don't work. Well, I should say the natural ways we deal with anxiety don't. At best, we delay the anxiety. At worst, we push it down and give it a chance to fester and grow inside of us.

Now think about that same story in the context of fight, flight, or freeze. If you had to fit your response into one of those categories, which would it be?

I am a flier. I have been since I was a little girl. I'll never forget being at a haunted house with my dad and my Brownie troop. We were standing in line, listening to the screams of other people in the house. I saw a poster of a vampire—it wasn't a real vampire (and by real, I mean a real person posing as a vampire) or even a super-scary image. I think it was an outline of a vampire that, in my mind now, looks more like the Count from *Sesame Street*. But within moments, I was down on all fours, backing my way out of the house between the legs of other people in line. My dad didn't even realize it had happened until I had exited the building.

I could say the same has been true in my life as I've gotten older, and in deeper areas too. It's not just a reaction to a silly sense of fear. It's a reaction to worry, anxiety, and stress. At times when things feel hard or scary, such as conflict with a friend, I often disappear. I back out and avoid that friend, conveniently unable to get together. In the last few years, I feel like I'm finally learning to stay in the scariness and talk things through. Not haunted houses—not ever again—but the more important scary things. The things that matter. I actually believe all of us, in silly ways and in deeper ways, lean toward fight, flight, or freeze.

What about you?

Sometimes fight, flight, and freeze are what are called involuntary reactions, which originate in the amygdala, the more reactionary part of the brain. But we also fight, flee, or freeze as a choice with the thinking parts of our brain, or at least the subconscious thinking parts of our brain. This kind of fight, flight, or freeze is more of a learned behavior than a survival reaction. It might have started as survival, but by now, it's gotten relatively entrenched.

Think of one story from your childhood that reflects a fight, flight, or freeze response. Write about it here.

Write about a more recent story.

_____

_____

_____

_____

_____

_____

Looking at those stories, do you think you're more of a fight, flight, or freeze kind of person? To get to where we're going, we have to start where we are. In other words, we have to start with an understanding of what doesn't help before we can get to what does. As we said in the beginning of this chapter, the fighting, fleeing, or freezing we do doesn't work—at least not for long.

The Path of Least Resistance

Fight

I'm writing this in the midst of a pandemic. Many businesses that were required by the government to close to prevent the spread of the virus are now reopening. At this stage, it's fascinating (and tragic as well, in terms of the loss that's occurred all over the world). In Nashville, we're required to social distance, wear masks, and gather in groups of fewer than ten. As you can imagine, though, that's not happening in lots of areas. In fact, it's making more than a few folks angry. I saw a sign outside of a restaurant that said something like "Open and should have been all along!" I think the owner must have been more of a fight kind of guy.

If it's hard to tell, think about your first reaction to conflict. And be honest about your first reaction. When someone confronts you about something, do you get defensive? Do you fire back, trying to explain your side? You may have heard the saying "The best defense is a good offense," which really means "Attack them before they can attack you." Can you relate?

What about your fears? When you're afraid of something, do you make yourself do it anyway? You're afraid of heights, so you're first in line to try the ropes course at camp. Or maybe your fight comes more in the form of sabotage. You actually set up the thing you're afraid of happening. For example, you're really afraid your two best friends are getting closer to each other than to you. Instead of talking about it, you tell them they should just go on without you, and you hang back to see if they'll try one more time to include you.

Sabotage doesn't work. You end up being left by the two friends you were afraid would leave you out. You get up on the highest pole of the ropes course and then realize you should have learned on the lowest. You end up hurt, and the thing you were afraid of actually comes true.

Flight

There are a lot of ways those of us who are flight risks choose to carry out our plans. The main three are denial, distraction, and escapism.

1. DENIAL

Denial and pretending could be the same idea. When we lean toward that method, we make statements like these:

"I don't really worry about things. I just get a lot done."

"I'm not rechecking the lock because I'm worried. It just makes me feel better."

"I don't want to think about it. I'd rather think about the good things."

With younger kids I'm counseling who lean toward denial, I take them outside and bring a Coke bottle with me. They're typically girls who are in the middle of their parents' divorce or something

66

else hard and anxiety provoking. We sit outside and talk about how "great" things are at home and school and in their lives in general, and all the while I shake the Coke bottle. At the end of the conversation, I open it—and Coke spews out everywhere. To deny or pretend is the same. We squash those feelings down and squash those feelings down, but they have to come out sooner or later. Often, they spew out all over your mom or little sister. Or they come out in the form of headaches or stomachaches. If you're a deny-er, you know exactly what I mean.

2. DISTRACTION

My counselor referred to this as brain candy. It was one of those sessions when you're not sure you even like counseling, because they tell you something hard about yourself. But in the long run, you're glad. In fact, I think it's part of our job, as counselors, to help you see the parts of yourself that you might not want to. Otherwise, you keep doing the things that don't work, and that ends up hurting you in the long run.

What he was saying was that I can get into a routine of work, brain candy, sleep. Work, brain candy, sleep. I wonder if the same is true of you sometimes. School, brain candy, sleep. School, brain candy, sleep.

He didn't actually tell me what brain candy means. (That's another sign you have a good counselor—when what they say makes you connect the dots on your own.) Here's my interpretation. Brain candy is something that's appealing and fun and distracting, but too much of it makes you sick.

What would be your distracting brain candy? Mine often is TV. Or playing a silly game on my phone. Or Mexican food. Or Coca-Cola. Now, candy is not a bad thing, and none of these things are either. But when I lost the first dog I ever had and really loved, all I did was cry and drink Coke. Somehow, Coke was comforting for me, but it wasn't helpful. I wasn't eating, and I wasn't drinking water. Just downing Cokes through my tears. Not terrible. Just not helpful. A lot of brain candy is like that.

What are your most common types of distractions?

_____

_____

_____

_____

_____

Then there's the brain candy that is more on the terrible side. I'd use the word *destructive*. I hear about that kind of brain candy in my office too. Alcohol, drugs, pornography—anything that can be addictive. Eating disorders are also a destructive form of distraction that quickly becomes addictive. Again, anything we do that's for the purpose of distracting us from our feelings can become destructive and only works to distract us for a little while. The feelings just come back after the distraction is over, and sometimes they come back with more destruction in their wake.

3. ESCAPISM

Escapism is a harder one. It's harder because it's often something you're taught. And I'm not at all trying to call your parents out here, but you may have to respectfully tell them it's time to do something different.

I'll never forget the time I saw a mom teach this form of flight right in front of me. I was walking through the Daystar lobby with Lucy on my heels. Let me just say, so you can put yourself in the scene, that Lucy weighs nine pounds. She's approximately ten inches tall. She's more fluff than form, but don't tell her that. And she's eleven, so she's missing most of her teeth. She is NOT an anxiety-provoking dog, as dogs go. Again, don't tell her I said so. She thinks she's quite scary. As Lucy and I were walking through the lobby, a little girl started screaming. I looked around to see what could possibly be wrong when I realized she was pointing at

Lucy. Her mom snatched her up, held her daughter's face to her chest, and yelled at me, "Keep that dog away from us!" She was teaching her to escape.

What I wish her mom had done is get up and walk over to Lucy, even leaving her daughter at a safe distance on the couch. I wish she had crouched down (way down, since Lucy is so small and not scary) and petted Lucy, saying, "What a nice dog." I wish she had modeled what it looks like to face your fear—not fight it, but face it.

But we run from those fears every day. I didn't take speech in high school because I hated speaking in front of people. (Ha—now I speak in front of thousands of people for my job. God's kind of ironic that way.) And often, when trying to help us, our parents help with the escaping. In fact, research says that the most common responses to fear and anxiety are escape and avoidance.[1] Of course your parents love you and don't want to see you in distress. And honestly, it's kind of nice for you not to have to be in distress.

Maybe you don't like to be away from your parents, so you don't spend the night at a friend's house. Or go to youth retreats or summer camp, even though you've always kind of wished you could.

Maybe you don't feel like you're a great athlete, so you stopped playing team sports where you could let the others down if you didn't do well. Now you've stopped playing sports altogether, but you feel a little like you're missing out.

Maybe you get anxious in crowds, so you have pulled yourself further and further out of the social world of your peers. Now even going to school is hard.

If you're escaping in this way, my guess is you already know what I'm about to say. Proverbs 13:12 says, "Hope deferred makes the heart sick, but a longing fulfilled is a tree of life." Any time I've pulled myself out of a situation because I was afraid, which I have done plenty, I've been sad about it later. Now, I'm not saying you should be doing all of the things all of the time and be under that kind of pressure again. I'm specifically talking about something you secretly want to do but don't because you're anxious.

What is one thing you haven't done out of fear that you regretted later, even if you've never said it out loud?

I believe all of us feel the best about ourselves when we're doing hard things. Not all the hard things, but a few along the way. We feel best when we're not letting our worries and anxieties prevent us from being who we can be. Courage brings confidence. But courage may feel impossible right now. It may be that you've pulled yourself out of enough things that you don't think you're capable of much.

Anxiety is an overestimation of the problem and an underestimation of yourself, remember? There is a better way, and it's coming.

Freeze

If you lean toward the freezing side of things, you likely feel helpless. You see the scary thing looming. The closer it gets, the heavier your feet feel. You know you need to get the research paper done, but the deadline just passes you right by. You just can't seem to make yourself do it. You're not necessarily escaping or avoiding. You're just paralyzed in a way that only makes you sad or frustrated with yourself later.

I also see another phenomenon happen often in my counseling office. It's when girls freeze more by choice than out of genuine fear. Maybe they do have some genuine fear at first, but the attention they get from that fear becomes more appealing than the confidence they would get if they worked through it.

"I have anxiety" or "My anxiety has been really bad this week," these girls say, almost as if it's a badge of honor. Undoubtedly, there are girls who make those statements out of their own sadness and vulnerability, asking for help and wanting to share their struggles with others. However, for some girls, it's not a source of pain, although they can make it sound that way. It actually becomes a source of pride. For these girls, anxiety isn't something to fight. It's something that has become part of their identity. It becomes a way others might pay more attention, or even see them as unique. They're allowing it to become a part of who they are.

Your primary job in these years—and for many more years to come—is to figure out who you want to be. You're defining yourself. It's part of that circle you drew in the second chapter. How do you want to define yourself? Have you thought about that question?

I want you to define yourself by the gifts that God has given you. Yes, you may be anxious, but you are braver than your anxiety. I know that to be the truth.

You may be sad. Depressed, even. You may have to be on medication for the anxiety or depression you're experiencing. It still doesn't define you.

Don't let something that's temporary have the power to be permanent.

Don't let something that's a small part of who you are define the sum total of who you are becoming.

Don't let a place where you've gotten stuck become a place where you live.

I want you to define yourself by more. I want you to define yourself by the things you're passionate about, the strengths God has given you, the things and people you love, the things that make you light up. I want you to define yourself by how deeply loved you are by a God who never wants you to be defined by anything less.

One of my all-time favorite quotes is "You are the only you this world will know, and something about your life is meant to make something about God known in a way no one else can do."[2]

When you're living in a frozen place—or are fighting or fleeing—you aren't getting to experience the only you God made. You're not free in the way you can be, even in the midst of this anxiety-producing world. There is a better way.

The Less-Traveled Path

"The Road Not Taken" by Robert Frost was my favorite poem when I was your age. . . . Still might be. Have you read it? It ends with "I took the [road] less traveled by, and that has made all the difference."[3]

I really do believe that this book—well, not so much this book as your bravery in the fight against worry and anxiety—can make all the difference. I believe it can free you to be you.

Throughout the next section of the book, we'll be talking about practical things that can help. We'll be talking more about the Worry Whisperer's most common tricks and your best tools in the fight.

All of the tools are ones I use daily in my counseling office. Many of them are adapted from a type of therapy called cognitive-behavioral therapy, or CBT for short. CBT is the most widely re-searched type of therapy for anxiety.[4] It works. But here's the thing: You have to practice.

From all of my years of counseling and all of the research I did to write these books, I think the most important thing I have learned is this: To work through your anxiety, you have to do the scary thing. And you've got to practice doing the scary thing over and over and over.

You're not going to do it without help. We're going to do this gradually and together, and I'm going to teach you lots along the way that will help in your fight against the Worry Whisperer.

Remember, he's a liar, but he's smart. He's going to try to come at you on every level. First, he's going to come after your body, where he tries to make the panic take over and set off all kinds of false alarms. Next, he's going to come after your mind, trying to make you believe that you can't do this. He's wrong. Finally, he's going to come after your heart. He's going to try to convince you not to do the scary thing. That you're not ready quite yet. That you're not capable. He's going to fight you hard, but you are brave, bright, and more than capable. He doesn't stand a chance.

But you will only beat him if you practice. Can we just go ahead and make an agreement? I'll teach you everything I know to help you fight Mr. W. W., but you've got to agree to try and to keep trying. He's had a lot of years to convince you that his voice is true. It's going to take more than a minute to convince yourself that it's not and for you to experience the freedom that's coming and the confidence that can come when you're taking the less-traveled path.

You've got this.

What are some of the things you've learned so far?

_____

_____

_____

_____

_____

What would you tell a friend who's struggling with anxiety?

_____

_____

_____

_____

_____

A Few *Brave* Things to Remember

- Most of us lean toward fight, flight, or freeze when we get anxious. These reactions can happen involuntarily or by choice.

- Fighting means we jump headfirst into whatever we're afraid of, including sometimes setting up the very thing we're most afraid of.

- Fleeing means we do everything possible to avoid the thing we're afraid of. We flee by denial, distraction, and escapism.

- Freezing means you've either been paralyzed by or allowed yourself to become stuck in your worry and anxiety. It feels like it helps to worry and be anxious. The problem is that it only helps in the short run.

- We feel the best about ourselves when we're doing hard things. Not all of the hard things, but a few along the way. We feel best when we're not letting our worries and anxieties prevent us from being who we can be. Courage brings confidence.

- CBT is the most widely researched type of therapy with anxiety. The CBT tools in this book will help, but only with practice.

- To work through your anxiety, you have to do the scary thing. And you've got to practice doing the scary thing over and over and over.

Section Two

Help

4. Help for Your Body

Let's pretend again that you're sitting in my counseling office. I'm in my cozy counseling chair, and you're on the couch, with Lucy sitting next to you. Actually, she's not sitting. She's waving. Have I told you that Lucy waves? It's her best trick—she holds up her little paws and waves on command. And not on command too. If we were in my office, she'd be waving at you right now, trying to get you to pet her or get me to get up and give her a treat. She does that at the beginning of every counseling session, which can sometimes be more than a little distracting. Okay—back to our session. I'm in my chair. Lucy has calmed down and is cuddled up right beside you.

I want you to tell me more about the last time you got anxious. Picture the scene. Think about what was happening around you. Where were you? Who was with you? Was there any conversation taking place? What did you hear? What did you see? Now think about what was happening inside of you. When do you remember the anxiety taking over? What did it feel like in your body? What did it do to your emotions? What did you do next? How did you work through it? *I want you to write the answers to those questions below, just as you would if you were talking in my office with Lucy and me.*

_____

_____

_____

_____

_____

_____

_____

_____

_____

_____

_____

The more we learn about the Worry Whisperer's ways, the easier it is to fight him. In this section of the book, we're not only going to break down his ways, but also what you can do to help. We'll talk about the Worry Whisperer's best tricks and your best tools to use in the fight.

We've already established several things about the Worry Whisperer:

- He's a liar.
- He's an isolator.
- He's confusing.
- He's smart, in a sneaky kind of way.

Part of his sneakiness is that he's going to try to come after you on several fronts. We traditionally think of anxiety as an emotion, but it's very much of a physical thing happening inside of our brains and bodies too. It's part of what makes it so confusing and hard to tell that it's truly the Worry Whisperer. He comes after us before we even recognize that it's him.

The Worry Whisperer's Tricks for Your Body

A False Alarm in Your Brain

I want you to hang in there with me, because we're going to have a little science lesson for a minute. Consider this Anxiety Brain 101.

When you and I are sitting here in my office (we're still pretending), we both have blood flowing throughout our brains, including to an area called the prefrontal cortex. The prefrontal cortex is what helps us do a lot of important things, such as think rationally and manage our emotions. Next, I want you to imagine something that frightens you. Say someone interrupts our quiet conversation, banging on the door and screaming. The blood flow in your brain would change immediately. The blood vessels would constrict, shifting the blood away from the prefrontal cortex and to the amygdalae. The amygdalae are two tiny almond-shaped regions toward the back of each side of your brain. The amygdalae work as a unit, so for our purposes, we will refer to them as one—the amygdala. But it's good to know that there are two, doing double duty together to store and interpret emotion. The amygdala has several purposes. It is connected to anger, aggression, fear, and even bonding with someone you love. The amygdala doesn't think or reason. It reacts. In fact, it reacts before your prefrontal cortex even has time to think, and it is the perfect playground for the Worry Whisperer.

If someone did that, interrupted our time and started banging and screaming, what would you do? Jump up and run across the room? Scream yourself? I'm sure that Lucy and I would both jump toward the door to try to protect you, although I'm not sure either of us is very scary. But there it is again. Fight or flight. Freeze too. The amygdala is the part of your brain that reacts immediately (within a fraction of a second) with a fight, flight, or freeze response.

God designed you that way. Rather than something being wrong, it's a survival instinct. In fact, you have this amazing sympathetic nervous system that comes online when your amygdala is activated. When it does, several things happen:

- It increases your heart rate.
- It increases your breathing rate.
- It increases the blood flow and glucose to your muscles.
- It decreases your digestive activity.
- It dilates your pupils.

You truly are fearfully and wonderfully made. God designed your body to respond to threats and keep you safe. In less than a second, He is using the amygdala to get your body ready to run faster, fight harder, and even see the enemy better.

The problem is that the amygdala is notorious for false alarms. The amygdala attaches emotional significance to situations and forms emotional memories. A psychologist named Catherine Pittman says it's like adding a Post-it Note to a memory.[1] Have you ever had a reaction to something that wasn't truly a threat? I think I have a very overactive amygdala, which means I have a high startle response. I scream way too easily. I embarrass myself lots. In fact, I often round the corner quickly at Daystar and scream when I see a co-worker. Of course, the co-worker is not a threat. Somehow, though, my amygdala has attached a Post-it that says when someone comes up on me quickly, it's dangerous. My amygdala is wrong. Yours is, at times, too.

Write about a time when your amygdala sent you a false alarm.

_____

_____

_____

_____

_____

_____

_____

_____

Amygdalae are helpful in dangerous situations, but they're not to be trusted. In chapter 6, we're going to talk about the only proven way to retrain the amygdala. For now, though, we just want to calm it down. We can't train it if we can't calm it down. Unless that calming happens, our bodies soon join the chaotic chorus of the amygdala, and then we (or our bodies) are really in trouble.

A False Alarm in Your Body

In this section of the little girls' book, there is a cute outline of a girl in a superhero cape. I tell the girls to draw a picture of where they first feel anxiety in their bodies on that little superhero. In fact, it's one of the first questions I ask girls of all ages who worry when I meet them.

I have little girls who tell me their tummies start to hurt. Some tell me their hands get clammy. Others tell me their chests get kind of tight. One girl told me she felt it first in her bow. Not sure on that one, but it sounded awfully cute. Most girls your age talk about having stomachaches or headaches. Some have talked about feeling light-headed and having trouble breathing. One girl even told me that her math problems would kind of swim in front of her when she got anxious during a math test.

What about you? If you had to draw in your outline of a superhero (which is you, by the way), where would you first draw the anxiety? Why don't you draw yourself in a superhero outfit here and write in where you feel anxiety and what it feels like?

It's important to pay attention to how anxiety affects your body. The amygdala doesn't communicate in words but in the physical sensations it creates. The bummer is that the amygdala really can cause you to feel sick. The headaches and stomachaches are real, even though your doctor may have told you that there is no medical basis. And now not only are you having headaches or stomachaches, but you feel panicked about getting panicked because of how bad it makes you feel. The great news is that we can make it stop. We can't necessarily make the anxiety-provoking situations stop; those are just part of living in a fallen world, a world this side of heaven. But we can quiet the false alarms that anxiety causes. We can stop the anxiety-provoking situation from having so much power in your brain and body. The earlier we can stop the process, the easier it will be to fight the Worry Whisperer on all fronts. Because, as you know, the longer the alarm sounds, the farther its reach. And pretty soon, it's not just our brains and our bodies reacting, but it's our emotions too.

An Emotional Siren

Alarms are loud. They don't go off without wreaking some degree of havoc. Your amygdala is just the same, and it likely has been since you were little. I meet with lots of parents of anxious little girls. The two things these parents say to me the most are these:

1. She is SO emotional. Most often angry, but there are tears too. Definitely tears.
2. When she gets that emotional, there is no way I can talk her out of it.

Maybe you remember. Your mom would tell you that it was time for bed when you thought you had thirty more minutes. You would try to convince her that you needed more time and suddenly find yourself on the floor, screaming. Or she would brush your hair for dance, and she just could NOT get those bumps out of your ponytail and it made you mad. Your parents were right—once you were upset, there was no talking you out of it. At that point, your alarm was going off with a lot of emotion and likely a lot of noise. Do you remember? Your homework right now is to go ask your mom or dad if they remember you having meltdowns when you were little. What would cause them and how did you behave during a meltdown?

What about now? When do you get the most emotional? Is it because of something you don't expect or can't control?

Anxiety loves control and hates unpredictability. Your amygdala kicks into high gear when your parents tell you to do something right away, when you thought you had more time. Or the plans change when you weren't expecting them to. Maybe you still hate change or surprises. I see girls who don't even like Christmas or birthday gifts, because the gifts don't end up being what they expected. It's not that they're spoiled or don't like the gifts they received. They just had one thing in their minds, and it ended up being something different. Unpredictability.

As a little girl, when those things happened, you likely had a meltdown. As an older girl, you likely get disappointed and cry in your room, or your anger quietly builds. Quietly, that is, until . . .

Our brains react. Our bodies jump on board. And our emotions quickly fall in line. When you were little, they fell in line loudly. Your emotions were more explosive in nature because you didn't know what else to do. Sometimes you still explode, mostly at your mom or dad or a younger sibling, and you feel terrible about it afterward. But I would guess that these days, you're more likely to implode than explode. You may get angry, but you're silently yelling at the person in your own mind. Or maybe you're not yelling, but you're being critical. Or maybe you only feel comfortable saying critical words about yourself. The emotion is still there—it's just directed inward, rather than outward. And that kind of emotion, anger especially, is destructive when it's directed at anyone, including you. I once heard someone say that anxiety is anger turned inward. I think panic attacks can often be described that way too. They have to do with pressure we feel to some degree, but I think they're also related to the anger we feel toward ourselves when that pressure is mounting.

The problem is that, whether the issue is little or big, whether you're exploding or imploding, the amygdala isn't reasonable. Your parents couldn't have talked you out of your anxiety when you were little. And you can't talk yourself out of it now—at least, not without the right tools. The false alarms really are just too much. And it feels like there is nothing that you or anyone else can do to fix it.

That's another one of the Worry Whisperer's lies.

If you could change anything about those times, what would you change?

_____

_____

_____

_____

_____

_____

_____

_____

We are going to get there. First, though, we need to understand a little more about the long-term impacts of a faulty alarm. With time, a faulty alarm just gets more faulty. The amygdala gets less trustworthy, and the longer that alarm goes unchecked, the harder it is to reset.

A Faulty Alarm

Do you know what the most common cause is for the false alarm? Worry. The Worry Whisperer, in other words. And chronic worry not only makes the alarm more likely to go off, but harder to turn off as well. It causes the amygdala to enlarge and develop what's called a hair-trigger response. Robert Sapolsky, a stress expert and professor at Stanford University, says, "Chronic stress creates a hyper-reactive, hysterical amygdala."[2] *Uh-oh.*

Would you consider yourself a chronic worrier?

Here's what happens, according to two psychologists:

> The actual physical architecture of the brain adapts to new information, reorganizing itself and creating new neural pathways based on what a person sees, hears, touches, thinks about, practices, and so on. . . . Where attention goes, neurons fire. And where neurons fire, they wire, or join together.[3]

In normal person's language, what that means is this: Your brain creates well-worn paths, just like the path between your house and your best friend's. You learn those paths by heart. You don't think about whether to turn right or left when you come to this street or that. You just know the way. Your brain learns certain ways by wiring neurons together and creating well-worn neural pathways. When we practice worry, even inadvertently, we wire those worry neurons together. When we practice bravery, which we'll talk about more in chapter 6, we wire those neurons together and create new neural pathways. We also retrain our hysterical, hyperreactive amygdalae. Isn't that great news?! We'll come back to exactly how to do that soon. But it really is important for you to know that worry has an impact. And chronic stress or worry has an even worse impact.

Here's something especially important for *you* to know: "Animal studies have found that after a prolonged period of stress, the adult brain will tend to bounce back within ten days, while the adolescent brain takes about three weeks,"[4] according to authors

William Stixrud and Ned Johnson. Your brain feels the residual effects of stress and worry. It's got enough on its plate already in these years with all of the learning and growing it's doing. We don't want to add to the stress. We want to practice using the tools instead. You can do this. You ready?

Brave Tools for Your Body

Before we get into the specific tools to fight the Worry Whisperer in your body, I want to remind you of two foundational tools: UNDERSTANDING and DETERMINATION.

Again, I wish we were sitting together. If we were, I hope you would have had a few "aha moments" so far. That you would have said things like "Oh . . . that's what was going on when I was so afraid of throwing up" or "I had no idea that my anger really had to do with worry." Or even "Now I understand why I would get so upset when I was little." I hope that this understanding helps you feel more understood yourself. I also hope it brings you a sense of relief—and of grace. The amygdala has been hijacking your brain for quite some time. The Worry Whisperer's tricks have been working. It's time for it to stop, which is where that determination kicks in.

Have your parents ever called you stubborn? I hope so. You're going to need that stubbornness now. You're going to have to be determined in this fight, even when it feels like it's not working. Even when it feels like you fall right back into the Worry Whisperer's ways. He's not going to win. But your brain has created well-worn paths. Creating new ones takes a little time, a lot of determination, and the right tools.

Know Your Triggers

When do you get most anxious? I want you to think back on ten times you've gotten anxious in the past few months, or even years. List those here, and then list beside them any themes, such as change or unpredictability. Also notice if they happen in similar situations or locations.

The more we can anticipate anxiety, the earlier we can start the fight. So let's start with paying attention to the where of worry. Then we'll move to the how.

Listen to Your Body

Go back to the drawing you did before. Where do you first feel the worry in your body? That knowledge is one of your most important tools in the fight. The amygdala takes over within less than a second, as you know, but those milliseconds are crucial. The longer we give the Worry Whisperer power, the stronger he becomes. Sooner is stronger for you. You want to start fighting him when you first feel his attempts to take over. Sooner is stronger. Where does he start with you?

Breathe

The first thing I want you to do when you feel him coming after your body in the place you named above is to BREATHE. I know, you're already doing it. But he's telling you to do it faster when he takes over, which will only make things worse. I want you to SLOW DOWN. In fact, there's a specific way I want you to breathe, and we're going to practice together now.

Put your hand on your leg and draw a square with your finger. As you slowly draw the first side of the square, breathe in. As you draw the next side, breathe out. Keep doing this until your square is complete. Research says that it takes six seconds for the chemicals being released in your brain by the amygdala to dissolve.[5] That's about one and a half squares. I would make it a four-square rule, though. It will give your brain time to reset (and it's easier to remember because, you know, foursquare).

Let me go ahead and say that I used to think all of the deep-breathing hype was kind of silly. That is, until I really tried it. I sometimes speak in front of several thousand people at once, and I still get pretty nervous. I will often stand over to the side and do square breathing before I go on stage. Or I'll do it when I'm having a conversation with someone and start to feel frustrated. It really does help—with worry and with anger too. Here's why:

Breathing is actually nourishment for your body. There are several cool things that happen when you take deep breaths. One is that the blood vessels in your brain dilate again, which enables your blood to flow back to your prefrontal cortex. In other words, you can now think clearly and manage your emotions. Also, breathing from your belly in particular kicks off this amazing series of events. Do you remember the game Mousetrap? It's a little like that.

You breathe deeply from your belly. Your lungs expand and press on your diaphragm wall. The diaphragm pushes your abdomen out and also pushes on your back, putting pressure on your spine. The pressure on the spine puts pressure on something called the vagus nerve, which happens to be the longest cranial nerve. It reaches all the way to your brain. This pressure quiets the vagus nerve and turns on the relaxation system of the body. In other words, it lowers your blood pressure, heart rate, and breathing rate. It also removes something called lactate from your blood (which increases feelings of anxiety), and it increases alpha brain waves, which are related to a sense of calm alertness. It even releases serotonin, which is connected to feelings of enjoyment, contentment, and impulse control.[6] And there you have it. Mousetrap that brings you back to a place of calm and being able to regulate your emotions . . . all from a few square belly breaths.

Grounding Games

It starts with breathing. Any time your brain is stuck in the worry loop, I want you to start with breathing. Basically, breathing is the most important tool in your toolbox, because, as you can tell, none of the other tools will work until your brain can reset. It's not capable of logical thought until then.

So you've reset your brain with square breathing. Now we need to get you out of the loop. One of my favorite CBT techniques is called grounding. There are several of what I refer to as "grounding games" that I use in my office with girls.

You may have noticed that worry lives in the past or future, not the present. The thing that's looping in your brain is usually either something that happened that you keep rehashing in your mind OR it's something coming up that you keep playing out because you feel anxious. Worry doesn't live in the present—which is exactly where you need to be. Grounding games do just what the name implies. When you're anxious, it's like you're free-floating over your body in some other time frame, and these games grab you by the ankles and pull you right back to the present.

My favorite grounding game is called 5-4-3-2-1. Let's play it now. In this game, you're going to use all of your senses:

What are five things you see right now?
What are four things you hear right now?
What are three things you feel right now?
What are two things you smell right now?
What is one thing you taste right now?

As you answered those questions, your focus was re-centered on the present. The senses do that for you. It's part of why I like square breathing as a way to deep breathe. The sensation of drawing a square on your leg is grounding in itself. Plus, you can do it sitting at your desk at school—or over to the side of a stage before you walk on—and no one will notice.

Other grounding techniques include colors and words:

Name everything you see that's the color blue.
Name every word you can think of that starts with the letter *R*.

Or you can do math:

Count backward from a hundred by sevens. (I know that's hard. You can do it.)
Do as many times tables as you can remember.

You can also run cold water over your hands, which is a great one at home or even at school. Talk with your parents about asking your school to let you leave class briefly to go to the bathroom for the cold-water-hands trick when you are anxious. Grounding games re-center you by requiring focus. Focus pulls you out of the loop of your anxious thoughts and back to the present.

Mindfulness and Memorizing Scripture

Another word you've likely heard in the past few years is *mindfulness*. Mindfulness is similar to grounding, but while grounding techniques pull us out of the loop and bring us into the present moment, mindfulness is more about paying attention to the moment without judgment. Grounding techniques are great to practice when you're looping and anxious. Mindfulness is helpful at any point. In fact, there are some great apps out there to help you practice mindfulness. Two of my favorites are Calm and Headspace. (Some of the apps out there, however, can get a little funky when it comes to faith, so if you'd like to try one, maybe check it out with the help of an adult you trust, such as a parent, counselor, or youth group leader.) Even simple belly breathing is a form of mindfulness. Mindfulness involves focusing on what's around you, what's happening inside of you, even a word or phrase.

I think one of the best mindfulness exercises we can do is to memorize Scripture. In fact, it's another thing I would have you do pretty soon after starting counseling. Actually, why don't you stop reading and start now? *Find a verse you love about worry. You pick. I want it to be something that brings you peace and comfort. Write your verse here.*

Now I want you to memorize that verse. You can practice mindfulness by saying the verse over and over and over any time. Focus on the first word, then the second, and just pay attention to where your thoughts go as you're doing it. Don't judge your thoughts—the Worry Whisperer would love to get you offtrack in that way. If you get distracted when you're practicing mindfulness, that's okay. Don't get mad at yourself. With mindfulness, you're supposed to let thoughts pass by like waves on a beach. You can even picture them that way in your mind. So say your verse to yourself over and over—when you're worried and when you're not.

I just sat here for a minute and practiced mine. I picked Philippians 4:6–8 (ESV):

> Do not be anxious about anything, but in everything by prayer and supplication with thanksgiving let your requests be made known to God. And the peace of God, which surpasses all understanding, will guard your hearts and your minds in Christ Jesus. Finally, brothers [and sisters], whatever is true, whatever is honorable, whatever is just, whatever is pure, whatever is lovely, whatever is commendable, if there is any excellence, if there is anything worthy of praise, think about these things.

God's Word changes us. I'm sure you've heard that before. It does not return void, meaning it always comes back bringing something with it. Just from my few minutes of reading that verse and meditating on it, I noticed something I haven't ever noticed before. "Peace . . . will *guard* your hearts and minds in Christ Jesus." God's peace guarding your heart is exactly what I want for you—and for me—as we fight the Worry Whisperer. I also saw another version that said, "Meditate on these things"[7] rather than "think about these things" at the end of the passage.

God's Word tells us to meditate. To meditate on Scripture is, in fact, scriptural. It strengthens our faith and our brains. Just eight weeks of practicing mindfulness, according to research, not only decreases amygdala activity but actually makes the amygdala smaller.[8] How cool is that? Memorizing and meditating on Scripture changes our hearts and our brains. It brings peace in the moment and strengthens our faith for the future. But there is one more thing you might have to do before you get to that peace.

Move

There are times when breathing just won't work. Neither will mindfulness or playing grounding games. You can't focus on a verse, let alone memorize it. Your anxiety has made you antsy and agitated. No thoughts going by like waves on a beach. They feel more like a frog dodging traffic. In those moments, it's time to move!

Just twenty to thirty minutes of exercise a day has been proven to reduce anxiety,[9] which is amazing in itself, but movement also resets the brain, much like breathing. So when you can't breathe slowly or do some of the more thoughtful practices, get outside. Go for a walk. Jump on a trampoline. Run. You may need to release some of that energy before you're able to do the activities that will get you out of the loop. In fact, you can do them at the same time. Walking and belly breathing, for example. You could take a mindful walk (or run), where you pay special attention to all of the sights, sounds, and smells around you. I don't know if you've ever tried yoga, but it involves movement, breathing, and mindfulness. Moving will also give you something else that might be important in your anxious agitation:

Space

If I were meeting with you for counseling, I'd also be meeting with your parents. One of the things we'd talk about is what they can do once your amygdala becomes activated. Honestly, it has more to do with giving you space than anything.

Let's say you and your parents got into an argument last night that made you anxious. Maybe they told you that you weren't going to get to attend a concert you've been looking forward to, because you had to go visit your Great-Aunt Ethel. You cried a few tears. Your volume got louder. Their volume got louder. Then it was hard to breathe. The Worry Whisperer had taken over by way of your amygdala. And their amygdalae jumped right into the mix.

It's time for space. In fact, what I would do with you all in counseling is come up with a code word. When either one of you said that code word, it would mean that you take a break. Each of you would go to your own room, or to a certain space to calm down. Maybe it's your room. Maybe you go for a run. But you each go somewhere you're able to process your emotions and calm your amygdala. Because basically, once your amygdala starts talking to their amygdalae, nothing good happens. Two amygdalae never have productive conversations. They don't use words, only reactions, remember? It becomes like a tennis match—you react, and then they react. Back and forth and back and forth until the problem is bigger than it was when it started, and you're likely grounded (and I'm not talking about grounding games).

Talk with your family about a code word and about the concept of space. Tell them I recommended it. Then I want you to come up with something that I wish every girl your age had hanging up in their room or in the notes on their phone.

Coping Skills

I want you to think, for a moment, about emotions on a 1 to 10 scale. *When was the last time you went to a 10?*

_____

_____

_____

_____

_____

What helped you calm back down?

_____

_____

_____

_____

_____

Whatever it was is actually a coping skill for you. One of the best things we counselors ever do is help you realize what coping skills work best for you. My guess is that you already know what they are. I want you to list twenty of your favorite coping skills here. They can be coping skills that are productive, or not so much. Include a few of both. Maybe don't include scrolling through social media or eating or things that can sometimes end up hurting more than they help, or even get us into an addictive situation. *But what makes a difference for you when you're at a 10—whether it's a worried 10, a sad 10, an angry 10, or any other kind of 10?*

_____

_____

_____

_____

_____

_____

_____

_____

Sleep

Yes, I said it. And you need it. You need it even in the midst of final exams. You might especially need it after a sleepover. Sleep deprivation increases activity in the amygdala. In other words, the Worry Whisperer is a lot louder when you haven't gotten enough sleep. I've noticed that sleep makes me feel better physically and emotionally. Getting a good night's sleep is sometimes the only thing that gets me out of a funk. According to the Anxiety and Depression Association of America, sleep "recharges your brain and improves your focus, concentration, and mood."[10]

Studies say that you need between nine and nine and a half hours of sleep per night in your teenage years. Do you know how much studies say that you get? Between seven and seven and a quarter hours.[11] That's not enough. What would you say you average? Research also says—you know what I'm about to say—you need to get off screens at least an hour before you go to bed. Sorry, but it's one of those things that really is backed by research. When you keep looking at your screen, the light keeps your brain from producing the melatonin that tells your body it's time to go to sleep. So you have a harder time falling asleep and are often more restless once you get there. "Sleep is brain hygiene," says Dan Siegel, a psychologist I really respect.[12] He says that when we don't get enough sleep, "the glial cells that are crucial for cleaning up the neurotoxins that build up in our brains . . . can't do their jobs."[13] The toxins just stay. Inadequate sleep also

- impacts our focus,
- impairs our memory,
- lessens our ability to problem-solve, and
- affects our insulin, causing us to gain more weight from what we eat and to eat more.

I don't know about you, but those things make me want to get more sleep.

Dan Siegel, along with a guy named David Rock, have another idea that I think is really important for us both. They call it a healthy mind platter. It's a little like the food groups you learned about in science, but it's for your mind. David Rock says these are the "seven daily essential mental activities for optimum mental health."[14] I would also say they're seven activities that help keep the Worry Whisperer quieted down. They're what we could call preventative practices in this war against worry. I wrote about them in the book for your parents (if your family routine changed after they read that book, now you know why).

Here's what was in their book:

Focus time is time that your daughter spends focusing on specific tasks, which challenge and give her brain opportunities to make connections. Schoolwork would be a primary place for her to have focus time. Learning or practicing a skill is also focus time.

Play time . . . strengthens her problem-solving and cognitive abilities, at the same time decreasing stress. In play, she uses her executive functioning skills in planning the play, and she uses a whole host of other skills, such as adaptability and intentionality, in executing it. It also teaches her to handle frustration and creates more flexibility. . . . So play not only lowers her stress in the short-term but teaches her skills to prevent stress in the long-term.

Connecting time is time for your daughter to relate to others and the world around her. Relationships strengthen the connections in her brain and help her discover more of who she is. Connecting time can be with family, friends, pets, or nature. All are important to her growing body and mind. . . .

Physical time is a significant deterrent and antidote to anxiety. Exercise releases endorphins, which are neurotransmitters produced in the brain that reduce pain. Exercise also increases the serotonin in her brain, which is often known as the "happy chemical." Over thirty minutes of exercise yields the greatest results. . . .

Time in is basically time for your daughter to reflect. This time can include mindfulness but cannot include screens. It's where she has space for the creative and reflective thoughts that kids need to de-stress and to grow. Having quiet time, reading, writing, and creating through art are all examples of time in.

Down time is non-focused time. It's the deliberate doing nothing and "being bored" that . . . is a rite of passage for kids. Down time is an important part of children learning to entertain and problem-solve for themselves. It's also often the first to go in a busy schedule. . . . This time is lying in bed before sleep, relaxing in the bath, sitting on a swing in the yard. Down time recharges the brain's batteries and helps it "store information in more permanent locations, gain perspective, process complicated ideas . . ." according to Stixrud and Johnson.

Sleep time is needed for optimal brain growth. Anxiety is worsened by frequent sleep deprivation. The authors of *The Yes Brain* explain, "Adequate sleep is necessary to allow the inevitable toxins of the daytime's neural firing to be cleaned up so we can start the day with a fresh, cleaned-up brain!"[15]

Now let's go back to my office. I want us to create a pseudo report card for your healthy mind platter. Here's what I want you to do: *Write the type of time in the first column and the hours you think you spend each week doing them in the second.*

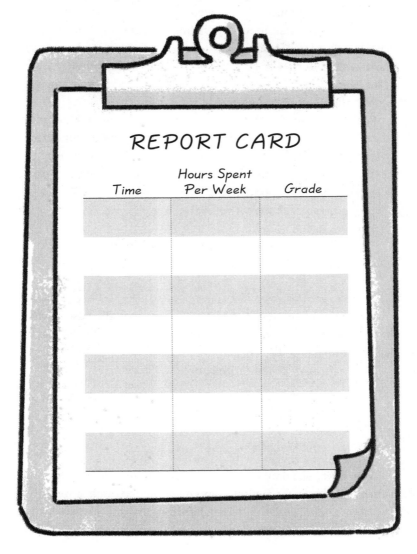

REPORT CARD

Time	Hours Spent Per Week	Grade

Next, I want you to go back and give yourself a letter grade on each type of time. How's it going? Mine is honestly not so great. I'm more of a focus and less of a physical kind of a girl. I literally felt so convicted writing about this that I just got up and walked Lucy for thirty minutes. I also needed to reset my brain because I was getting anxious about my writing deadline and how much I have left. It helped. I came back fresh. All of us could improve in these areas, but they're good goals. And they're preventative. We want to continue to think about preventative practices we can use against the Worry Whisperer.

Really, we want three types of practices: preventative, immediate, and lasting. We covered the preventative and immediate practices in this chapter. You know what to do preventively to keep your amygdala and body in a healthy place so that the Worry Whisperer has less opportunity.

Name three of those things here:

You know what to do in the immediate to stop the false alarms in your brain, body, and emotions so that the Worry Whisperer has less impact.

Name three of those things here:

Now let's talk about change. It's about more than just prevention or help in the moment. It's about learning to think differently. It's about being freed up from the thoughts that can so easily consume our minds and our hearts and keep us from being who we want to be. It's about lasting change. And that change is coming. Keep reading.

What are five things you've learned in this chapter you want to remember?

_____

_____

_____

_____

_____

What are five things you would tell a friend?

_____

_____

_____

_____

_____

A Few *Brave* Things to Remember

- It's important to pay attention to how anxiety affects your body. The sooner you catch it, the easier it is to stop it. And the more you learn about worry's ways, the easier it is to fight it.

- The first place the Worry Whisperer comes after you is your body. He hijacks your amygdala, which reacts with fight, flight, or freeze. To beat the Worry Whisperer, we have to start by calming down the amygdala.

- The more frequently the amygdala sets off a false alarm, the more likely it is to do so. Your brain gets better at whatever it practices, including worry.

- Your best tools to fight the Worry Whisperer in your body include knowing your triggers, listening to your body, breathing deeply, playing grounding games, practicing mindfulness and memorizing Scripture, moving, going to your space, using your coping skills, and sleeping.

- Deep breathing resets the amygdala, calming down the false alarm.

- Grounding games help pull you out of the worry loop and bring you back to the present.

- Mindfulness helps you focus on what's happening around and inside of you. Memorizing and reciting Scripture gives the added benefit of calming your worries AND reminding you of truth that can fight those worries at a much deeper level.

- Coping skills help you find outlets to express your worry and whatever emotions might be lying underneath it in healthy, constructive ways.

5. Help for Your Mind

Several years ago, I went to a conference on a counseling topic. I can't remember what it was anymore. I guess it didn't make a lasting impact. But out of the six hours I spent sitting in that auditorium, there are five minutes I do remember.

The man leading the conference had just started speaking. He was introducing himself and talking about his credentials when a woman loudly entered the auditorium. When I say loudly, I mean she was hollering from the moment she walked in and continued as she marched down the aisle and right onto the stage with him. Honestly, at first, I thought she was crazy. She was shouting things like, "What business do you have being up there? You don't have anything helpful to say. They're not going to listen to you. You don't even look like you know what you're talking about, let alone sound like it. You should have just stayed home." I'm not kidding. She was saying these things to the man leading the conference loudly enough for everyone to hear. I was shocked. And so was he, obviously. At first, he was kind to her, saying things like, "Thanks for your thoughts on that," and he would try to keep talking. Then he started nervously saying, "I'm not sure you're in the right place. I'm going to need you to sit down." The more she came after him, though, the more he shrunk back. By the end of her tirade, she had taken center stage and he had faded into the background.

What do you think happened next?

I was on the edge of my seat. She stopped, smiled, and introduced herself to the audience. She said, "I'm the voice in your head."

Wow.

In other words, she was his Worry Whisperer. She sounded a lot like mine too. Probably yours as well. Her words were representative of what his thoughts sound like once the Worry Whisperer has taken control.

The Other Pathway to Worry

Let's have another quick Anxiety Brain 101 lesson. In the body chapter we talked a lot about how the amygdala region of your brain impacts your body. The amygdala is one pathway to anxiety. It's the path that's taken when the person is banging on the door to my office. We could call it the Worry FastPass. With the Worry FastPass, the false alarm sounds in the amygdala, the sympathetic nervous system kicks into gear, and logical, rational thought goes out the window. The prefrontal cortex is shut down and you're in full-blown looping anxiety land. It all happens in less than a second. There's no thinking. There is only reacting that temporarily turns off thinking.

But there is another path the Worry Whisperer takes. It's the path that starts with thoughts. It involves the cortex, which includes your prefrontal cortex. The cortex is what you traditionally picture when you picture the brain—all of that gray, squiggly matter. It has lots of regions and lots of functions, including memory, language, creativity, judgment, attention, and emotion. And it's another path the Worry Whisperer can use to get to you.

The cortex path is different from the amygdala. The cortex path starts with a thought—often an intrusive thought.

I wonder if I'm going to get sick.
I wonder if someone I love might get cancer.
I wonder if I'll fail my test.
I wonder if my friends are mad at me.

Write down three thoughts you've had lately that are these kinds of worried wonderings.

The thought comes out of nowhere. Or maybe it comes out of a perception or misperception, which we'll come back to later. We all have dozens, or potentially even hundreds, of intrusive thoughts per day.[1] On a good day, those thoughts just drift right by, like waves on an ocean. Or they do that when we're practicing the mindfulness exercise that helps us send them drifting by like waves on an ocean.

But on certain days—or for some of us, during certain hours in a day—they take hold. We stop and notice those thoughts, ruminating on them (which we'll come back to later as well). Basically, they get stuck. Then those thoughts kick-start our amygdala onto its well-worn path to trouble.

The amygdala is always involved, unless we can teach our cortex to override it, which is the goal of this chapter. But just like we talked about in the last chapter, we've got to learn the Worry Whisperer's tricks to better understand where to fight him. And again, sooner is stronger. So let's start with what he does when he comes after your very smart and capable mind.

The Worry Whisperer's Tricks for Your Mind

The amygdala reacts. It impacts our brain, our body, and our emotions and pretty much creates chaos in all of the above. The Worry Whisperer is actually fairly obvious to track down in those areas, which makes it easier to shut him down with the right tools. But he's sneakier in the cortex. He comes after the ways we think . . . which only take place inside of our head. And if we're not careful, those voices inside of our head will be voices we believe as truth.

> The cortex is where we anticipate . . . believing we're preventing problems before they happen. This kind of anticipation is really just dread.
>
> The cortex is where we ruminate . . . believing we can think through whatever scenario that might present itself. But this kind of rumination is really just overthinking that quickly turns into obsessing.
>
> The cortex worries. I'm not sure how we think worrying will help, but we do it anyway. This kind of worry really just exacerbates and prolongs anxiety.
>
> The cortex is where we hear the voices of criticism, rejection, doubt, and guilt. It's where we hear that things aren't complete, that things aren't okay . . . that we're not okay.

The cortex is just another area where the Worry Whisperer lies. He's wrong—once again. But until we learn to recognize his voice, we will believe it as truth.

Anticipation

Most anxiety happens before an event ever takes place. And the worry over the event is usually worse than the event itself. It's called anticipatory anxiety. We could just call it dread. I have a friend who wakes up every day with a sense of dread. I hate it for her. Her first thoughts are about all of the bad things that are likely to happen that day. I playfully call her Eeyore. She has those "slight chance of rain" kinds of thoughts more often that she would like.

106

The thing is, for anyone who struggles with anxiety, the *slight chance* of rain means that it *will* rain. Possibility becomes a high probability. The Worry Whisperer shifts fear to fact.

"You will fail your test."
"You will have a panic attack at your next track meet."
"Your mom will get cancer and then die."
"Your friends will betray you."

It's called an exaggerated likelihood. You're not just worried about the bad thing happening. You're certain of it. The Worry Whisperer makes you feel like the bad things are inevitable and that you should just go ahead and prepare yourself for the worst. And then it sure feels like the worst happens.

When you find yourself in a state of dread, I want you to ask yourself the following question: "What really is the likelihood that this is going to happen?"

Perception

I know a girl named Sophie who struggles a lot with friends. I've known Sophie for about six months, and I honestly can't figure out why she struggles in that area. She's delightful. She's smart and creative and funny and kind. The only thing I've been able to come up with is that she's just too mature for her years and her peers. They don't get her. So I decided to put Sophie in group counseling so she could find some girls who do get her.

Sophie started group counseling and tried really hard with the other girls. They responded immediately with enthusiasm. I could tell they liked her. They even talked about getting together outside of counseling. Week after week, Sophie would ask great questions of the girls. One week, she approached me after group and said that the girls didn't ask her very many questions back. I thought about it, and she was right. What she thought was that they didn't care. What I knew as a counselor was that they were just being narcissistic teenage girls (although kind ones). They did like her. They just weren't as good at asking questions.

A few weeks later, Sophie told me that no one had reached out to get together with her after they had mentioned it in group. She thought they didn't like her after all. What I knew was that it was the spring semester and these girls all had too many activities on their plates, and they were just narcissistic teenage girls (yes, still kind).

Several weeks went by again. Sophie's dad called me. Sophie felt like the other girls didn't like her. She said they would walk right by her and not speak when they came into group counseling and leave without saying good-bye. She thought that not only did they not like her, but they didn't want her to be in the group. What I knew, as a counselor, is that they do the very same thing to me. Sometimes I walk in and say, "Hello, everyone," and when they don't respond to me, I just go ahead and say, "It's time for you to now say hello back to me." It's not that these girls don't care, it's that . . . yep, they're kind, narcissistic teenage girls.

The problem wasn't the girls, although I do feel for you, as a teenage girl. Honestly, it's pretty normal for girls your age to be narcissistic—so normal, in fact, that in a book I wrote with my friend Melissa, *Raising Girls*, we called these the "narcissistic years" in a girl's life. But that can make it hard to find true friends. The problem wasn't Sophie either. The problem was Sophie's perception. It was her interpretation of the event. That perception, in turn, was giving Sophie social anxiety. I don't think it was happening only in that group. It was likely happening in all of her friendships, which was why she was struggling. She had the thoughts and trusted that those thoughts were true. Her dad did too, which gave Sophie's thoughts even more power. And let me tell you—Sophie's real name isn't Sophie, obviously. Sophie isn't even just one person. She's more like twenty. I have probably seen twenty girls over the years with the exact same story and same trouble, and that trouble started in their cortexes.

The cortex is constantly interpreting events. Those interpretations become our perceptions. And our anxiety is directly proportional to our perception. In relationship, our perspective is skewed because, as girls, we believe we can read others' minds. It's what all of the Sophies were doing. Their perception of events was based on their interpretation of how those girls felt about them. I think most of us do that. We believe we know exactly why someone is acting a certain way, and it's usually skewed negatively against us. It's not true. And I hate to be the one to break the news to you, but you can't read others' minds. Neither can I, and I've been trained in it.

Perception, however, isn't just mind reading. It's also situation reading.

She's mad at me.

I failed that test.

I blew that audition.

I'm not as good as everyone else at ____.

Our perception makes us believe things are true when they're not. Mark Twain is quoted as saying, "I've lived through some terrible things in my life. Some of which actually happened." It's not the event. It's the thoughts the Worry Whisperer creates out of our perception that lead to anxiety. Don't confuse thoughts with reality. There is always more to the story.

Write about a time when you decided, based on your perception, that something was true that actually wasn't.

When you catch yourself falling for the old perception trick, whether it's mind or situation reading, I want you to ask yourself: "Could there be more to the story?"

Rumination

An article from the *Atlantic* says, "The habit of what psychologists call rumination—essentially, dwelling extensively on negative feelings—is more prevalent in women than in men, and often starts at puberty. This can make girls more cautious, and less inclined toward risk taking."[2]

While thinking through this chapter, I kept accidentally swapping the words *rumination* and *marination*. I think they're really one and the same. You've probably helped someone marinate chicken before. *Marination* is basically soaking a food in a certain liquid before cooking. *Rumination*, according to writer and leadership expert Rachel Simmons, "is defined as repetitively focusing on the causes or consequences of a problem."[3] In other words, rumination means we're not just soaking, but swimming around in negative feelings or thoughts. It's overthinking at its best, it's not helpful, and it makes anxiety and depression worse. In fact, research says that it is a "well-established risk factor for the onset of major depression and anxiety symptomatology in adolescents and adults."[4]

I hear girls talk about this very idea daily in my office. "I'm an overthinker." You know it if you do it. You think through something on the way to school that you're worried about, and sometimes it starts in a productive way. Then you find yourself thinking about it in math. It's quickly getting less productive. And then while driving home. And then, again, when you're supposed to be doing your homework and when you're lying in bed at night. The productive thoughts have turned into unproductive rumination.

Here's something else to consider: Co-rumination compounds the problem. *Co-rumination* has been defined by the

American Psychological Association as "excessively talking with another person about problems, including rehashing them and dwelling on the negative feelings associated with them." In a six-month study with over eight hundred girls and boys participating, co-rumination, for girls, led to closer friendships but also increased anxiety and depression. I think it's important to point out that the study used the words *rehash* and *pattern of co-rumination.*[5]

Obviously, as a counselor, I believe it's important for you to think through and talk about your feelings, including feelings that you might consider negative. Sharing your feelings is one of your biggest tools in the next chapter. It's important to talk with your friends about your feelings. But you know when thinking turns into overthinking and talking turns into rehashing. You can feel the difference. Talking brings a sense of relief. Rehashing just creates more frustration and despair.

I've seen this very phenomenon many times. I call it the helicopter effect. A girl starts talking, and the helicopter leaves the ground, helping her feel better and lighter. There is a point, however, where the pattern of rehashing begins. She talks over and over about the same problems, and the helicopter comes right back down to crash on the ground. Think through and talk about your struggles. Share in each others'. But rumination becomes overthinking, which becomes obsessing. We want to get those negative thoughts and feelings out, but we don't want to spend so much time on them that they just circle back around and make us feel worse. Can you think of a time when talking actually made you feel worse? Can you think of a time it made you feel better? What was the difference?

If you have a friendship that might be the co-ruminating kind, talk about it together. Hold each other accountable and come up with a gentle way to remind each other when the co-ruminating begins. Friendships are meant to lighten our load, not pile it higher. The Worry Whisperer loves a good pile on, and the bigger it gets, the worse it feels and sounds.

Catastrophization

Do you remember our definition of anxiety? Anxiety is an overestimation of the problem and an underestimation of ourselves. Catastrophization is the overestimation part of things.

It's not only bad, it's the WORST EVER!

It wasn't just scary, it was TERRIFYING!

It wasn't just sad, it was DEVASTATING!

It wasn't just annoying, it made you want to LOSE YOUR MIND!

How many times have you said one of these phrases, when really just the first part of the sentence was true? It's so easy for any of us to do. And it comes more naturally for a few of us. Even your parents might do this. I read a study that talked about how anxious parents use more catastrophic language when things go wrong.[6] They might say, "She fell and almost broke her arm," when really you just stumbled and scraped it. But it's easy to end up doing the same thing. Sometimes it's fun to make the story a little bigger. Sometimes it might get you a little more attention. And sometimes it's just the way you see it.

Maybe you're more prone to big feelings. Maybe you're a little more sensitive. Or a little less resilient. And so small problems are perceived as big, and big problems as insurmountable. And we've circled right back around to perception. When we catch ourselves using ALL CAPS language, it's good to ask questions like "Am I catastrophizing?" and "Is this really a small problem, a medium problem, or a huge problem?" If we're not careful, the Worry Whisperer will take our tendency toward catastrophizing and turn it into our perception of reality.

It's another story I've heard play out countless times in my counseling office. The first time I ever heard it was from a girl who was afraid of cheating. She was taking a test in class and had an intrusive thought. *I would never want the teacher to think I was cheating. I need to be careful where I look.* (Anticipation.) That thought took hold in her cortex. *Oh no. I just looked around. Now I'm sure my teacher thinks I was cheating.* (Perception.) *I don't want to cheat. I don't want to cheat.* (Rumination.) Her cortex then scared her amygdala. *What if I already did? Oh no, I cheated. Oh no, I cheated.* (Catastrophization.) Then she didn't feel like things were right until she confessed to the teacher that she had cheated. This bright, conscientious girl had never cheated in her life.

I've seen the same thing happen about a whole host of subjects from thoughts of wanting to hurt someone to sexual thoughts to thoughts of suicide, none of which were what the girls actually wanted. Specifically, I have had a lot of girls over the past few years tell me that it's not that they would want to kill themselves. It's that they're afraid of killing themselves, so they can't stop thinking about it. If any of the above are true about you, it's really important that you tell your mom or dad or a counselor. You're too important to even consider that idea without talking to someone who can help, worries or no worries.

Catastrophizing is an overestimation of the problem that can take us from thinking of something to believing it's going to happen. Actually, it's not just going to happen, But it's going to be the WORST when it does.

Underestimation

Now we've passed the problem and come to the you part of our definition. It's no longer about the likelihood, or your perception, or how terrible the problem is. It's about you at this point. And you can't do it. You can't handle it. You're going to fail. An overestimation of the problem and an *underestimation of yourself.*

The problem is not only too big, but you're too small. In all of these years of counseling, I have never met a girl who doesn't struggle with this idea in some area of her life.

What are your areas? Where do you feel incapable?

What are the messages the Worry Whisperer sends you when he makes you feel that way?

_____

_____

_____

_____

_____

_____

_____

_____

There's not a lot more to say about underestimating other than that it's a lie. And this is where I would go back to calling the Worry Whisperer by his true name—the Father of Lies. You are capable. Now, when I say the Worry Whisperer is lying and that you are capable, my guess is that you're arguing with me some inside of yourself. That's okay. Let's talk about that.

I truly believe that God has given you everything that you need—not just around you, but inside of you. Philippians 4:19 says, "And my God will supply every need of yours according to his riches in glory in Christ Jesus" (ESV). To me, that means if you don't have it, either (1) He's still growing it in you or (2) you don't need it.

There are certain things you aren't—you know that already. There are certain things that I'm not too. Some of those are still growing in me, like patience. Maybe you're not funny. Sometimes I wish I was funny, but I'm not—unless it's by accident. I could try to work on it, but I still just wouldn't have it. I'm also not super athletic. It's not that I'm being hard on myself. It's just a fact. I'm not capable of certain things athletically that others are. I am a pretty good water-skier and have been since I was little, but I am not a good tennis player, and I've tried that since I was little too. We all have different strengths. That doesn't mean God hasn't given me everything I need. He's given you everything you need too.

I think my favorite passage in the entire Bible is this: "My dear children, let's not just talk about love; let's practice real love. This is the only way we'll know we're living truly, living in God's reality. It's also the way to shut down debilitating self-criticism, even when there is something to it. For God is greater than our worried hearts and knows more about us than we do ourselves. And friends, once that's taken care of and we're no longer accusing or condemning ourselves, we're bold and free before God!" (1 John 3:18–21 THE MESSAGE).

"Even when there is something to it," to me, means that sometimes there's a little truth to some of the things I'm critical of myself about. I'm not very funny. I'm not super athletic. And that is okay. I don't need to be, and I certainly don't need to worry about it.

Let me stop and say, for your parents' sake, that if you're not good at math, that doesn't mean you throw up your hands and say, "Oh, well. I'm not good at math." Some things are just not our gifts, but some things are more like muscles. Patience is one for me. Math might be one for you. There are still muscles we can work on. But what all of that means is that you can be free of underestimating yourself. God has given you everything you need. He has given you exactly what you need to be able to do the thing He's put in front of you. He wants you to feel bold and free before Him! You can do it.

Forgetfulness

Worry has no memory. In my research, I read that statement over and over. It's one of the Worry Whisperer's very favorite tricks. And as a counselor or someone whose job is to cheer you on and remind you of how brave you are, this trick makes me crazy! And I'm not catastrophizing. It does because he's wrong.

When you go to do your next brave thing, he's going to pull out all the stops. He's going to make you think the problem is bigger, that you're smaller, and that you have never done anything brave before. Even if you did something really brave yesterday or five minutes ago. He loves to make you forget. That's one of the reasons this book is as much journal as it is book. I want you to remember. *In fact, I want you to write down three brave things you've done recently below:*

_____

_____

_____

_____

_____

_____

You are brave. You are stronger than any worry that comes your way. And the sooner you recognize his voice and his favorite tricks, the easier it will be to beat him.

Which of these tricks does the Worry Whisperer use the most with you?

_____

_____

_____

_____

What specifically does he say?

_____

_____

_____

_____

I want you to remember those statements so you can recognize him the next time he comes. And I want you to start using your tools to beat him in your mind.

Brave Tools for Your Mind

> We demolish arguments and every pretension that sets itself up against the knowledge of God, and we take captive every thought to make it obedient to Christ.
>
> 2 Corinthians 10:5

Taking captive every thought. I sure like that image. It sounds like we're beating that lying Worry Whisperer. He is arguing, pretending, catastrophizing, ruminating, and setting himself up against the knowledge of God . . . against the truth that God would want you to hear. But we can take every one of his argumentative thoughts—and those tricks—captive and make them obedient to Christ.

Science backs up Scripture—isn't it cool when that happens? Taking every thought captive is possible, not just from a spiritual standpoint, but from a neurological standpoint. Have we talked about the word *neuroplasticity* yet? It's basically a smart-sounding word that means that your brain is still growing. We start by taking the thoughts captive that are really the Worry Whisperer's tricks, and then we have the opportunity to learn new thoughts. To learn tools that will basically rewire your brain.

Remember when we said what fires together is wired together? You can change the circuitry of your brain by what you practice. We strengthen circuits by using them. It's not just immediate relief, like breathing and grounding, although we have to start with the immediate help to give our brains a chance to change. But when you practice taking those thoughts (tricks) captive and replacing them with new ones, you're literally changing your cortex. The cortex learns by education, logic, argument, and experience.

Research says that the best way to rewire the circuitry in the cortex is for you to practice the thoughts and interpretations you want to strengthen.[7]

The cortex is the much easier anxiety pathway to change. We're going to talk about changing the amygdala in the next chapter, but it's going to take more muscle than thought. For now, we want to focus on captive thoughts and a captive Worry Whisperer.

Expect Worry

I know—it sounds weird that expecting worry is a thought I want you to practice. But I do. Have you ever heard the definition of insanity that is "doing the same thing over and over and expecting different results"? I love that because it's helped me stop doing some of the same things over and over. It's helped mainly by changing my expectations. The goal for this book isn't for you to never worry again. I want you to expect worry.

There are going to be hard things that happen, which we'll talk more about in chapter 7. But you also worry because of your temperament, remember? You worry because you care deeply and are smart and conscientious and thoughtful. You will go through phases when the Worry Whisperer is louder and quieter—likely for the rest of your life. He'll be quiet for a period of time. Then when he resurfaces like in the whac-a-mole game, I want you to simply think, *Worry's back.* Not surprised. Not alarmed that something is wrong with you. Not that the *Brave* book you read when you were a teenager didn't help.

Know your triggers and expect worry. He'll be back, but you'll be stronger. The more you expect him, the more you recognize his voice when he resurfaces. Sooner is stronger. Every time. And next time, you'll know even better how to fight him.

Worry Time

Knowing that you're going to worry will help when the worries come. I always want you to remember, though, that you're stronger than your worries. So I want you to do something that's going to sound strange. Well, I want you to do it until the Worry Whisperer is captive again.

Set aside a time for worry. Yes, you read that right. Schedule a worry time. Scheduling worry does a few important things:

- It keeps you from pushing the emotions down so hard that they come out sideways as anger or even greater anxiety.
- It keeps you from feeling like you have to fight this battle perfectly, because I sure don't want to add to the list of things you think you have to do perfectly.
- It reminds you that you're in control of your worry. It is not in control of you.

So schedule a daily worry time, at least in the beginning as you're learning to take the thoughts captive. Don't make it while you're lying in bed, though, or it will be hard to stop and fall asleep. Make it on the way home from school, or at a time you when can just sit and think.

The CBT name for worry time is containment. It's a little like if you literally were taking a person captive. The first thing you would do is put handcuffs on them. Contain them. With worry time, you're putting handcuffs on your Worry Whisperer. Set a time that works for you. Talk through it with your mom or dad, if you'd like. At the end, I want you to pray. It's how we do the second part of 2 Corinthians 10:5. We take every thought captive and make it obedient to Christ. Pray and then get up and do something else.

Go for a walk. Read a book. Play with your dog. Talk to your parents. FaceTime a friend. The doing something else is called changing the channel in cognitive behavioral therapy. Give yourself a set period of time, pray, and then change the worry channel. When you do, you're teaching the Worry Whisperer that he's not in charge, but you and God are.

Find the Evidence

Have you ever read the Nancy Drew books? They were my favorite when I was growing up. This tool is all about bringing your best girl detective skills to the game. It's where we turn his tricks back on him and ask those questions:

Anticipation: "What really is the likelihood that this is going to happen?"

Perspective: "Could there be more to the story?"

Rumination: "Is my thinking/talking helping or making things worse?"

Catastrophization: "Is it really as bad as I'm making it out to be?"

Underestimation: "How prepared am I?" Or you could ask, "What would Sissy say about me now?"

Forgetfulness: "What have I done lately that's brave?"

So you've taken the thoughts captive, and you've made them obedient to Christ. And now you've proven them to be false. It's our own version of a fact check.

Name the Thoughts

Back in the first chapter, we gave the Worry Whisperer his name. Do you remember how we talked about him being like the mole in the whac-a-mole game? How he comes back in different ways as you get older, basically as the scariest thing you can imagine at that particular age?

I wanted you to name him so you would learn to recognize him as separate from you. Like we've talked about, it's the most natural thing in the world for us to think the voice in our head is true. When you learn to recognize that voice as the Worry Whisperer, though, you know it's not true. You know he's a liar. And when his voice is separate from yours, it doesn't have nearly as much power.

There's another reason I wanted you to name him. Because when he comes back, I want you to recognize him in whatever form he comes. I want you to be able to say, "Mom, that Worry Whisperer has been trying to get at me again lately. This time, he's bugging me about friends." Or college. Or whatever he thinks will most likely get you looping.

Here's the really great news: The same tools work. He picks new ways to try to trick you, but the tools you're learning now will work with whatever way he picks. It doesn't matter if it's about throwing up or failing a test. When he starts to tell you that the problem is bigger and you're smaller, you can respond by telling him exactly what he can do with those messages.

Boss Back

If you were sitting in my office, I'd scoot an empty chair up next to you. I'd have you pretend the Worry Whisperer was sitting there, and I'd have you say exactly what you wanted to say to him, using your strongest, most sarcastic voice. Okay, okay, I wouldn't really do that. That's a counseling technique we learn in graduate school called the empty chair technique, but it's not so much my style. I think I'd feel even more awkward than you would. But I want you to learn to do that in your head.

When he starts to bug you with his tricks, I want you to call the Worry Whisperer by name and tell him exactly what you think about him.

When he talks, I want you to talk back.

When he tells you that you can't, I want you to tell him that you can and to shut up.

When he tells you that you're a failure, I want you to tell him that he's failed. Again.

If he tells you that you've never done anything brave before, I want you to remind him of the brave things you remember. If he tells you that you're not smart enough, I want you to remind him of how wrong he is and how smart you are. With the little

girls, I call it bossing back. You can even flash back to your sassi-
est little girl voice and stomp your foot and shake your finger, at
least in your own head. Basically, I want to strengthen your voice
in this fight. I want you to know and experience that your voice
is stronger than his.

Psychology books call them coping thoughts. Let's call them
truth, because that's exactly what they are. You are stronger than
your worries. You're braver than any anxiety that can come your
way. He's going to do his best to tell you something different, but
your best is better. Practice. Take every one of his thoughts captive
and make them obedient to Christ and to the truth of who Christ
has made you to be. Those are the kinds of thoughts I want you to
fill your head with. They're the kinds of thoughts that can literally
change your cortex. They're the thoughts that will free you to be
the brave person that you are.

What are ten truths you can remind yourself of when the
Worry Whisperer starts talking?

Hang those truths up in your bathroom and copy them in your
phone so you can look back at them whenever his voice starts

to try to drown yours out. You are stronger, smarter, and braver. Don't forget.

What are five things you've learned in this chapter that you want to remember?

_____

_____

_____

_____

_____

What are five things you would tell a friend?

_____

_____

_____

_____

_____

A Few *Brave* Things to Remember

- The two pathways to anxiety are by way of the amygdala and the cortex. The amygdala reacts, and the cortex thinks. The cortex anticipates, ruminates, and catastrophizes, making those worried thoughts become not only our perception, but our reality.

- Worry is an overestimation of the problem and an underestimation of ourselves.

- We can take every thought captive (2 Corinthians 10:5), both spiritually, through prayer and memorizing Scripture, and neurologically, with tools from this chapter. Practicing the tools literally rewires our brain to reduce anxiety.

- Our tools for the mind include expecting worry, making worry time, finding the evidence, naming the thoughts, and bossing the Worry Whisperer back.

- The more you expect worry, the more you recognize his voice when he resurfaces. Sooner is stronger in your fight against worry.

- Set aside time for worry. That time will help you process your worry, but in a way that helps you know you're in control of your worries, rather than your worries being in control of you.

- Find the evidence against each of the Worry Whisperer's tricks. Are they true? How likely is the scary thing to happen, really? Use your detective skills to disprove his tricks and strengthen your confidence.

- Use your strong voice to talk back to the Worry Whisperer and remind him that he's not the boss of you.

6. Help for Your Heart

With each chapter of this "Help" section, we've gone a little deeper. We started with your body, where things are more automatic and more on the surface of who you are. They don't have a ton to do with you—just the way God designed your body to react to a threat. Then we went a little deeper and talked about your mind, the thoughts the Worry Whisperer tries to drop there, and how you can take those thoughts captive. If we were in counseling, though, I'd want you to keep going deeper. And by this time, I'd feel like I knew you well enough to try. I'd want to help you get out of your head and into your heart. Not just "What are you thinking?" but "What are you feeling?"

I told you this before, but I believe you're really kind. I'm not even sure that I've ever met a girl who's anxious and unkind. I think being kind is part of the deal. You care deeply about others. I think you feel deeply. I think you see and take things in that (1) others often don't notice and (2) others have no idea that you're seeing, noticing, and feeling. I think it's part of why you worry, but I absolutely believe it's something God wants to use.

Do you remember our quote about you being the only you? It's one that Melissa, who started Daystar, uses often, and I think it's one that bears repeating, because it's so true about you. "You are the only you this world will know, and something about your life is meant to make something about God known in a way no one else can do."[1] I think that "something about you" that God wants to use is your heart. And your heart is the last place the Worry Whisperer comes after you. It's kind of his last-ditch effort to defeat you. And I believe your heart is the most important tool you have in this fight, because it's the key to what this book is about: finding you.

This book *is* about being brave and learning to fight your Worry Whisperer. But more than that, it's about discovering the you that God made you to be . . . down deep in your heart. The Worry Whisperer is going to try to do everything he can to stop that from happening. I think he has a little inkling of the difference you're going to make in this world, so he's going to try one last place to stop it. But we're wise to his tricks. He just doesn't know it yet.

The Worry Whisperer's Tricks for Your Heart

"Anxiety is a method of seeking two experiences: *certainty* and *comfort*. The problem is that it wants these two outcomes *immediately* and *continually*," according to the authors of *Anxious Kids, Anxious Parents.*[2] Can you relate to that statement? This may sound a little brutal, but one of the things that I tell parents a lot is that anxious kids and teenagers are some of the most controlling people I know. Ouch. Sorry.

It's true of me too. We anxious adults are pretty controlling ourselves. We all want certainty, comfort, and control. If we can't find those things, we'll hop right on over to avoidance. And those are four of the Worry Whisperer's biggest tricks in his fight against your heart. The truth that we know is that none of them work for long. It sounds like bad news, but it's actually good. When we can let go of our drive for certainty, comfort, control, and avoidance, we find ourselves in a place that's wide open to what God wants us to experience. But I'm getting ahead of myself. First, we need to understand each of these tricks and why we believe our survival is dependent on them taking place. Or at least why the Worry Whisperer tries to make us believe that's so.

Certainty

I remember one of the things I hated the most when I was a little girl was when my mom would use the word *maybe*. I'd ask if I could have a friend over. "Maybe." I'd ask if we were going to see my grandmother, Hedy. "Maybe." I'd ask if we could go out to eat for dinner. "Maybe." I still remember the frustration rising inside of me at just that one word. I didn't want maybe. I wanted certainty.

It wasn't just because I wanted what I wanted, though that might have been the case a little. It was more because I didn't like the dangling unknown. I still don't. I have to stop myself from making plans weeks in advance and remind myself that other people don't seem to have the same need I do to know all that's coming. But I would guess that you might. Certainty makes us feel safe. When we know what's coming, what's expected of us, and how things are going to turn out.

Write out a few things you like to know.

_____

_____

_____

_____

The only thing is that we don't know. We can't predict the future, and it wouldn't help if we could. I'm going to let you in on a little parenting secret. One of the ways I tell parents they can recognize anxiety in their kids is when their kids ask endless questions. "What time are you going out? When will you be home? Who are you going with? What am I going to do while you're gone? *When* will you be home?" Those kinds of endless questions. You might have been an endless-question asker when you were little. I also tell parents not to answer more than five questions about the same topic. It's one of the things I learned in my research on anxiety. Answering every question doesn't help. It's not about the questions anyway. It's about certainty. In those Endless Question moments, the Worry Whisperer is telling you that if you don't have certainty, you won't be okay.

You've lived long enough at this point to know that certainty isn't always possible. You can be okay and not be certain of what's coming.

Comfort

In asking those questions, kids aren't just wanting answers and certainty. They're wanting reassurance. They're wanting their parents to respond in a way that brings comfort.

I know a girl named Anne. Anne is really smart. She's funny and kind and super enjoyable to be around. You'd like her. Anne also has panic attacks. She's a junior in high school and has panic attacks whenever she has to be away from home overnight. It happens on school trips. It happens before summer camp. She doesn't even like to have sleepovers with friends, because it happens then. We talked about it not too long ago in my office, and she said something I'll never forget.

"I realized recently that my mom and I are the closest when I have panic attacks. It's when she's the most nurturing to me. I hadn't thought about it before, but maybe that's part of it. It's not why I have them. But maybe it's why sometimes I don't stop myself from having them once they start, when I really do know how."

Anne has a great mom. She's strong and smart and funny—she's just not the most comforting mom in the world. But she is when Anne has panic attacks. Anne wants comfort, as we all do.

I know girls who find comfort in every area imaginable. I remember a girl who, when she worried, only found comfort if she touched things. She'd have to touch a book, and then she'd have to touch the table that the book was touching. Then, she'd have to touch the rug that the table was touching. I know other girls who have to tap on opposite sides of their bodies equally to find a sense of comfort. You may have some type of what is referred to as a ritual that brings you comfort when you're anxious.

I want you to think back for a moment about bedtime when you were younger. Did you have any kind of routine? I sure did. I would have my mom look under my bed and in my closet (because, you know . . . monsters). She would then sit on my bed, and we would have to say the same prayer the same way every night. Then I had to say, "Sweet dreams. God bless. Night, night. I love you." And she had to say it back. Every night. I had no idea at the time why we had to follow that routine, but now I understand. It brought me comfort when I felt anxious. Many girls I talk to wouldn't use the word *comfort*. They'd say things don't feel "right" until they follow a certain routine. It's not the same as feeling comforted by someone you care about when you're said—it's comfort in that those routines seem to hold our anxiety at bay.

We all have things we do that bring us that type of comfort when we're anxious. Maybe it's eating or exercising. Maybe it's spending time with a friend or petting your dog. Maybe it's a routine or some type of ritual. None of those things are problematic in themselves. The problem comes when we feel like we have to do it or we won't be okay. That's when anything can become more compulsion than comfort. And as you know, those compulsive rituals don't work for long either. Or maybe they work, but it becomes so complicated to do them that we end up more anxious than we started.

What are three things you believe you need or need to do that bring comfort?

You're okay. Right now and when you're anxious. And even when you don't have or don't do the thing you believe brings the most comfort.

Control

How would you say you do with unpredictability? What about change? If those are not your favorite things, then you might lean toward control or wanting to control. Control might sound like too strong of a word to you. I wouldn't necessarily say I want to be in control. I just don't want to be out of it. I don't do well with chaos. Even a lot of noise and voices and commotion is unsettling to me. Unless, of course, it's Disney World. Then I can take every bit of chaos that Mickey and Mary Poppins can throw at me.

Being in control involves both certainty and comfort. I know what's going to happen because I'm going to make sure that it does. I also know what brings me comfort and how to get it. I'm in control.

I remember sitting in a car on a date with a boy in high school and making myself wait for him to ask me a question. Silence makes me uncomfortable when I don't know the person very well, so I typically ask a lot of questions and keep the conversation going. I wasn't trying to be controlling or trying to dominate the conversation. I was trying to be kind, and I didn't want things to be awkward, but I think it might have come out as control.

I also hated group projects. If I could do the project by myself, I could do the work. I could get the grade I wanted—or at least close to it. But with a group, there was always that one kid who wouldn't do the work and you couldn't control him or her (but let's face it, it was usually a him). It still makes me frustrated thinking about it.

What are some areas where you find yourself trying to stay in control?

I'm afraid control is just like certainty and comfort. We can't actually control things, or we can't keep them under control for very long. Not if we live in a family. Or have relationships with people . . . both of which we do want to happen. But other people aren't under our control, no matter how much we try. Life isn't under our control. Control doesn't work either. And sometimes, the more control we get, the more controlling we become. And that's certainly not what we want.

You can be okay and not be in control.

The other problem with every one of those ideas is that we learn to trust the certainty, comfort, or control more than we trust ourselves. And I absolutely want you to learn to trust yourself. For now, trust me. We're going to get there. But we've got one more of the Worry Whisperer's tricks we've gotta talk about first.

Avoidance

Boy, do I see this one a lot in my office. And boy, do I see parents who unintentionally make the problem worse. Not long ago I met with a girl who was being homeschooled. Now, homeschool can be a really great thing, under the right set of circumstances. But unless the anxiety is so severe that a child physically can't attend school, the decision to homeschool should not be based on anxiety . . . which was exactly why she was being homeschooled.

"She was struggling with friends," her mom told me. "And so she started feeling sick at school. She'd call me every day after lunch to come pick her up. She really did seem to feel bad, so of course I did. Then she started getting sick earlier and earlier in the day, until she woke up feeling that way. It was just too much for her. So now we're homeschooling and she loves it. But I thought it might be good for her to come in and talk to someone about it. I think maybe she's anxious."

Maybe just a little. And maybe she got exactly what she wanted. I'm not saying she didn't feel sick or that she doesn't have anxiety. I think she does. But if they'd started counseling a little earlier, she could have learned the Worry Whisperer's tricks and her tools to fight him. She could have practiced before and while she was at school. I think it wouldn't just have helped her stomach, but also her heart. And I believe she would have felt better about herself for having beaten the Worry Whisperer, rather than avoiding him entirely. She was avoiding the thing that made her afraid, but she was also avoiding the Worry Whisperer. He won. Which means she, really, was the one who lost.

The more things get out of control, the more we go after certainty. And comfort. And right back around to control. If all else fails, we avoid. Avoidance actually strengthens anxiety.

What is something you're avoiding right now that you really wish you could do?

_____

_____

_____

_____

_____

Now, if you've done this very thing—you've pulled yourself out of something you were afraid of, even school, because you were afraid, I want you to say, "One win for the Worry Whisperer doesn't defeat me." He's beaten all of us at times. You can still do the brave thing and do it in small steps. The rest of this chapter is going to help you with how.

You're always going to feel better about yourself when you do the brave thing. And to work through your worry and anxiety, you're going to *have* to do the brave thing. The Worry Whisperer simply does not go away unless you face him. He just gets bigger and you get smaller. He doesn't have to, though. You can do this.

You can do the brave thing and be more than okay, especially if you use your tools.

Brave Tools for Your Heart

These tools—these heart tools—are about deep, lasting change. The tools for our bodies bring peace and calm in the immediate, which we need. The tools for our minds bring change in our cortex, which changes the way we think and matters a lot too. But these tools, these tools for your heart, will change the way you live. They'll help you learn to talk about your feelings in ways that create deeper relationship. They'll change the way you approach life and obstacles and create more confidence. They'll help you do the brave thing and enable you to discover more of you in the process.

Emotional Vocabulary

A psychologist named Paul Ekman said there are six basic emotions: anger, disgust, fear, happiness, sadness, and surprise. Another psychologist named Robert Plutchik named eight: joy, sadness, anger, fear, trust, distrust, surprise, and anticipation.[3] According to a study of our faces from Glasgow University in Scotland, however, we only register four: It found that fear and surprise share the same facial expression, as do anger and disgust.[4] Who knew?

My authority on emotions, however, says that there are five primary emotions. And their names happen to coincide with the emotion they represent: Joy, Sadness, Fear, Anger, and Disgust. Sound familiar? I'll give you another hint . . . "I would die for Riley."[5] Yes, I'm talking about the movie *Inside Out*. If you haven't seen it, I'd highly recommend it!

In the little girls' book, I have a feelings chart made of faces of Lucy, my dog. It's SUPER cute, but I thought it might be a little young for you. The girls are supposed to fill in the name of the emotion under each face. We included sixteen emotions on the chart: happy, sad, worried, afraid, angry, brave, hopeful, jealous, grateful, disappointed, embarrassed, excited, frustrated, uncomfortable, proud, and safe. I'm including your own feelings chart in the back of this book. I want you to look at it for a few minutes and think about the last time you felt each of those emotions. Go ahead . . . now is a great time.

How many of those feelings do you actually talk about with other people? With your family? Friends? I have a feeling you might live more on the happy, hopeful, grateful, excited side of things. Actually, it's not that you necessarily live there. It's that you express there. I know we talked a little about this before. I think it's part of your kindness. Most really kind girls I know don't know how to talk about their anger. They'll say to me, "No, I don't get angry very often." I think girls often have a harder time expressing anger, frustration, and sometimes even sadness and disappointment, thinking they won't be perceived as kind. Or good. Or likable. You feel every one of those emotions, if you would only let yourself. And there is not an emotion that's bad, or mean, or inappropriate, or even sinful. In fact, Ephesians 4:26 says, "In your anger do not sin." That means our anger is not wrong—it's what we do with it that can hurt us and others. The same is true of every emotion. As a friend of mine said, when we don't process our emotions, our emotions will process us. In other words, if we don't let our feelings out in healthy, appropriate ways, such as art or journaling or talking, our feelings will find their own way out . . . and often to the detriment of us and others.

In fact, I would venture to say that when you're not talking about your feelings, they'll find one feeling to use as their primary route. Mine come out mostly as anger and irritation. I will often find myself frustrated as I'm falling asleep. When I dig underneath that feeling, though, I realize that I felt hurt, left out, or worried at some point that day. Or maybe I hurt someone else. Only I didn't process it in a healthy way . . . or at all.

You might be more like a friend of mine whose feelings seem to prefer the anxious route. It happens for her when she's in the shower and in the car and when she's falling asleep too. It's those times when she's quiet and not distracted. Then all of a sudden, she realizes she's overwhelmed. Close to tears. Having trouble breathing, even. Her anxiety is processing her in those moments.

During the summer, we take our Daystar kids to a place called Hopetown. It's a beautiful home on the lake where we have our own version of summer retreats, complete with tubing and worship and talking—lots and lots of talking. My friend Melissa, who started Daystar, owns Hopetown. She also does all of the Bible teaching and is my favorite Bible teacher to people your age.

Several summers ago, she talked about something I'll never forget. She actually had the kids go sit in one of our vans in the driveway, and she talked about the importance of an oil light. She said that an oil light comes on as a warning signal. It's telling us that something is wrong underneath the hood of our car. When that oil light goes on, it's in our best interest to pay attention. Melissa compared our emotions to an oil light. I would add that each of our oil lights follows a certain pattern or emotion. They look a certain way. In the van that afternoon, she said that what we often do when our emotional oil lights flash, however, is ignore them. It's the equivalent of taking a hammer and shattering the light. Our car, and our hearts, suffer.

What's your emotional oil light? Circle one of the feelings below.

Anger	Sadness
Anxiety	Frustration
Despair	Hopelessness

I didn't even realize till now that I had an oil light.

The next time your oil light turns on, I want you to choose three additional emotions you are feeling—three that live under the hood of your heart in that moment. And I want you to write or talk to a friend about what's causing those emotions. I truly believe it will make your worry better.

I can't tell you how often I've had girls come in to see me and say their anxiety is worse than usual and that they "don't have any idea why." The longer we talk, the more I'll hear about one particular friend who has been hurting their feelings. Or I'll find out that their parents are getting divorced. And I can almost always assure you that, whatever is going on underneath the anxiety, they weren't talking about it with anyone in their life.

From an Anxiety Brain 101 perspective, talking helps too. Studies show that talking about our feelings actually reduces amygdala activation and stimulates the region of the cortex that helps with emotion and motivation.[6] How awesome is that? Now, let's talk about that motivation—or the things that get in motivation's way.

Brave Ladders

I would guess there are some things you'd like to do that your worry stops you from doing. Maybe they're things that you haven't really admitted to anyone else. But you know, down deep, you'd like to do them. Maybe you even feel like God wants you to, but your anxiety gets the better of you. Rather than trying, you spend your time avoiding. Avoiding doing the thing . . . avoiding even talking about the thing. Maybe you get defensive when it comes up in conversation.

If we were sitting in the same room, this is when I'd lean toward you. I'd want you to know I get it and am with you. I know it's hard. But I also know this to be true: Avoidance strengthens anxiety. It actually keeps the amygdala from learning. According to research, the only way to create lasting change in our amygdala is through experience.[7] We have to do the scary thing. The more you do the scary thing, the more resistant your brain gets to anxiety. It develops its own set of anxiety-fighting muscles. And that's exactly what we're talking about with this idea of brave ladders.

Let's pause for a moment. Before we get to the ladders, I want to start with thermometers. Here's a thermometer. If you had to rate your worry right now, on a 1 to 10 scale, what would it be?

Just for an experiment, do your square breathing four times. *Now where is your worry on the scale?*

The thermometer is a tool I want you to remember. We're going to come back to it as we use the ladders. I know—your English teacher would be mad at me for mixing metaphors. But whatever. It works.

Now I want you to think of something you've been wanting to do but haven't because you've felt anxious. Actually, I want you to think of five of those things. It may take a minute, and that's okay. They can be little or big. It could start with eating brussels sprouts or something silly . . . all the way up to going on a school trip. But they need to be things you want to do. It could be speaking in front of people. It really could be anything that's doable. Maybe, for now, don't pick hiking the Himalayan mountains or something that might be a little more complicated to pull off. *I want you to list five goals below.*

Now give each of your five goals a rating on your thermometer for how anxious you feel when you think about trying to achieve them.

Now let's pick the easiest one. The one that makes you feel the very least anxious. *On this ladder below, I want you to write the actual goal on the top step. Then we're going to think about the steps toward it.*

Steps can involve real life, or they can be in your imagination. In therapy terms, in vivo (real life) or imaginal (imagination) exposure therapy is what this is called. Now you sound official. Let's just say you're terribly afraid of dogs, but you really want one.

The top of the ladder would be getting a dog.
One step below that would be housesitting for a friend's dog.
One step below that would sitting on the floor and playing with a friend's dog.
One step below that would be holding a little dog.

One step below that would be sitting in the same room with a friend's dog, but not touching it.

One step below that would be going to a dog park but sitting outside the dog area.

One step below that would be watching videos of dogs on YouTube.

One step below that would be imagining yourself playing with a dog.

One step below that would be imagining a dog playing by itself.

If you're a tapper or a checker or someone who has some type of ritual that you use to help with worry, it can feel like things aren't "right" until you do the ritual. But that's your Worry Whisperer talking again. The more you perform the ritual, the more you live by his rules. A first step, in this situation, would be to not let yourself do the ritual. It's called response prevention, and it's an important part of silencing the Worry Whisperer. Exposure therapy is gradually working your way, step by step, to doing the scary thing without obeying any of worry's rules. There are, however, a few important steps with each step.

1) At the beginning, take your worry temperature.
2) You have to stay in that step until your worry temperature drops to half of what it was. It may take up to forty-five minutes or an hour. That's okay.
3) You have to do the ladder several times (at least three) for your amygdala to learn.

It's going to be hard. That's part of the point. You can do hard things. You can do these things and a whole lot more. Your amygdala is going to activate in the beginning. It has to. To learn new pathways in your brain, the amygdala has to be triggered. Breathe. Practice grounding. Do the things you know to do to help in the moment. But if your amygdala doesn't join the party, it won't learn.

Tolerating anxiety really does change anxiety, and as you work through it, you'll start to see truths like these:

I feel anxious right now, but it will get better.

If I stay in the scary thing, I won't feel as scared.

I don't like to feel anxious, but I can handle it. It won't hurt me.

My worry can't stop me.

This is uncomfortable, but I can do it.

I'm stronger than my fear.

Exposures create lasting change. You are literally rewiring your amygdala to respond differently, which is amazing. The more you work your ladders, the easier it will be. Think about the last time you did something hard. How did you feel at the end of it?

I once rode four hundred miles on a bike to raise money for Daystar. It was the hardest physical thing I've ever done. I cried every single day, but I did it. (I did laugh and enjoy my friends who were doing it with me and sing a lot too. It wasn't all uphill—just mostly.) I will forever be proud of myself for doing the brave thing. What's something hard you've done that made you feel proud? I want you to feel proud of yourself. To feel capable. To experience the bravery I know is inside of you. I also want you to experience a few rewards along the way.

Rewards

We need your parents for this tool. Seriously. I want you to ask them to read this chapter, and maybe even the parent book too, because it has a whole section on this. You're going to need rewards. I need rewards, still, as an adult. Even writing this book, I get up and get myself a treat from time to time or play with Lucy. Obviously, Lucy is the way bigger reward.

I want you to think of twenty things that would be rewards for you. You need little ones and big ones. Things that cost money and things that don't. Your parents will, obviously, have to be on board with these, but here are a few ideas:

Getting to pick where your family goes out to dinner

An extra sleepover with a friend

A sleepover on a school night

A sleepover with several friends at once

Your parents' paying for you and a friend to go to dinner

A new book

Going on a date with one of your parents

A new pet

A trip with one parent

Getting a manicure with your mom

Keep going. What else would feel like a reward to you?

Okay, so here's the plan. Go back over your list and give each reward a number value. Then, go buy yourself a big mason jar and some fun pompons or something similar from a craft store. Any time you take a step on your ladder, or do something brave, your parents give you a pompon. You may have to remind them that you earned one. Then you can work your way toward little and big rewards that you can "buy" with your pompoms along the way. The biggest reward of all, though, is going to be the confidence I know you'll find as you do the brave things. Okay, let's be honest—confidence and a new pet might be a tie in my book!

Practice

We've talked about how the two pathways to anxiety are also the two pathways to lasting change: the cortex and the amygdala. You rewire the cortex by replacing anxious thoughts with brave ones. You rewire the amygdala through experience. Both are going to require practice. And when I say practice, I mean a LOT. The number one reason that people don't work through anxiety is that they don't practice. Just like avoidance strengthens anxiety, anxiety left alone only gets worse. It's going to take time to create new pathways in both places. It's going to be hard at times. You're going to feel afraid. When you feel afraid, it just means the practice is working. Keep going. You can do this.

Problem Solving

Sometimes, it's not our worry that blocks us. It's someone else or our worry over what that someone else might think.
Maybe we'd offend them.
Maybe they wouldn't think we were nice anymore.
Maybe they'd think we were weird.
Maybe it would create more drama.
Maybe they'd no longer want to be our friend.

Years ago, a girl said to me, "Sometimes it's easier to let other people think for me than to have to think for myself." When we live in those kinds of maybes, that's really what we're doing. We're letting others think for us, AND we're letting others solve our problems. Or prolong our problems, depending on the person and on the problem.

I want you to find your voice.

Research says that problem-solving has been proven to reduce the likelihood of developing an anxiety disorder.[8] I would also say that for the girls I know, the problem is not a lack of problem-solving skills, but their lack of confidence in their problem-solving capability.

I have a feeling you might lack confidence in your own problem-solving capability. Or maybe you don't. At least, you don't when you're by yourself. But when you're around your friends, or boy-friend, or parents, even, it gets a little harder.

We girls are intuitive creatures. It's one of our best gifts—and just like those old 45 records, it's also one of our worst curses. We know when someone doesn't like something we've said. We know when someone might not like us. We usually know what others want us to say and how others want us to act. In those times and in those situations, it's especially easy for us to doubt ourselves and let others think and problem-solve for us.

I want you to find your voice.

If I had to say my goals for this book right now, they would be that you would find your voice and that you would find your confidence in your own problem-solving capability. But even more, I want you to trust that God's Spirit lives inside of you, guiding and giving you direction. His voice is there. You can often find His voice by the feeling you get in your gut—this little stirring deep down inside you that quietly hints at a direction to go. A choice to make. What to say in a certain moment. Who you want to be in a particular situation.

I want you to find your voice. I want you to trust God's Spirit leading you. I know way too many girls who don't. They don't believe their voice matters, and they don't trust and follow what they think might possibly be God's leading. So they live in the maybes. Here's a formula that I believe will help you find your voice when you encounter problems. I want you to ask yourself these questions:

1. What do I believe God would want?
2. What does it look like to love other people?
3. What does it look like to value my own beliefs and myself?
4. Who do I want to be in this?

I truly believe that if you answer those four questions, you'll find your voice. You'll find that gut sense of who God has made you to be and how He's leading you. My gut is honestly the thing I use the most as a counselor. When I'm sitting with someone in my office and feel like I have no idea what to say or do, I can often feel this little stirring inside of me. The older I get, the more I trust in that stirring. The more I believe it's God directing and guiding me. He wants me to find my voice, and He wants you to find yours.

The Worry Whisperer wants to stop you. He wants to silence you and stop you from doing the brave thing. From practicing. From listening to your emotions. From acting on those emotions. From using your voice. From finding and being you. That's really all this chapter is about. Listening to our hearts and acting on what they say. Doing the brave thing and believing God is leading the way, He has our good in mind, and He has already overcome the world and the Worry Whisperer. More on that soon.

In the meantime, I'm so proud of you. You've basically taught yourself some of the most important tools in cognitive-behavioral therapy. You're already retraining both your cortex and your amygdala, and you've done the brave thing by reading, thinking, and practicing. And using your voice, even in the pages of this book. I can't wait to see where you go next, especially as we talk about the hope undergirding every bit of understanding and help on this brave journey.

What are five things you've learned in this chapter that you want to remember?

What are five things you would tell a friend?

_____

_____

_____

_____

_____

_____

_____

_____

A Few *Brave* Things to Remember

- The Worry Whisperer's tricks for your heart include certainty, comfort, control, and avoidance.

- The Worry Whisperer tells you that you're not safe unless you're certain of what's expected, what's coming next, and all manner of things that none of us can really be certain of.

- The Worry Whisperer will try to convince you that you need comfort at all costs. *"Don't do the thing that makes you uncomfortable. Staying safe is the only way to get rid of your anxiety."* But the opposite is true: Taking risks and doing the scary thing is the only way to truly work through the worry.

- The Worry Whisperer tells us we're not okay unless we're in control. But it's not possible to be in control, so we live in a perpetual state of anxiety. The good news is that Someone much wiser than we are *is* in control.

- Avoiding the scary thing feels like the answer to worry and anxiety. But the scary thing morphs into another scary thing and another. And suddenly, we find we've given worry way too much power to limit and define us. Avoidance strengthens anxiety.

- Your brave tools for your heart include an emotional vocabulary, brave ladders, rewards, practice, and problem solving. You're always going to feel better about yourself when you do the brave thing.

- If we don't let our feelings out in healthy, appropriate ways, our feelings will find their own way out, often in the form of worry and anxiety.

- The only way to create lasting change in the amygdala is through experience—through doing the scary thing. Brave ladders are a way to do the scary thing in small, manageable steps, with lots of rewards along the way. The number one reason people don't work through anxiety is that they don't practice.

Section Three

Hope

7. Trouble

I want you to think back on being in fourth grade. Picture your little self sitting in church on a Sunday morning or in the gym for your homecoming pep rally. What were you wearing? Who were you sitting with? Now visualize the high school girls that you thought were the coolest in your school or church—picture them walking right by you. Can you see them? They were dressed so cute and looked so confident, like they didn't have a care in the world. They sure didn't look like they were experiencing trouble. And since they didn't look like they were experiencing it, you didn't expect it when you became a teenager yourself.

It's kind of like any time we think about the next stage of life:

When I get to middle school, things will be so much better.

At least when I get to high school, the girl drama will be over.

When I can move on and have a fresh start in college, I'll finally have real friends.

When I get married, I'll feel loved like I've always longed for . . . all the time.

When I have kids, I'll feel like my life has a sense of purpose.

And on and on and on. We don't expect trouble. Then we get there . . . wherever "there" is. And there that trouble is again—or a new type of trouble.

Until recently, I would have said you were a generation that didn't expect much trouble. I said to your parents at parenting seminars all over the country that it was mostly our fault, as grownups. We were wearing T-shirts and using hashtags that said "Livin' Our Best Life" and "Best. Day. Ever." I told the grown-ups in your life that I felt like we were doing you a disservice, because you didn't know to expect trouble. I told them your expectations were set so high that when something went wrong, you felt like something was wrong with you or with your life, rather than realizing that we all live every day in the midst of some kind of trouble.

These days, however, trouble is more visible for a lot of us. I'm sitting on my porch in the midst of a pandemic. People are walking by in masks, worried about the trouble that might come. In Nashville, we had terrible storms this spring. We've also seen horrific racial violence here and across the country. We're living in the midst of trouble like none of us have ever experienced. None of us were expecting this kind of trouble.

I want you to write five to ten things you were expecting to be true about your life when you became a teenager.

My guess is that those things are likely not what you are experiencing. Let's break it down a little more; now I want you to write what's true. *Take each of those expectations you wrote and write down what life is really like for you now, regarding that specific expectation.*

_____

_____

_____

_____

_____

_____

_____

_____

_____

_____

I don't know what you wrote, but I could guess based on thousands of conversations I've had with girls your age over the years. Again, you're not alone, either in how you're feeling or that you weren't really expecting things to be quite this way.

You were expecting to have grown out of the awkwardness you feel inside, but you still feel that awkwardness rear its head way too often.

You thought you'd know who you are, but you are still falteringly figuring it out.

You were expecting to be confident, but you're still unsure. A LOT.

You were expecting to be surrounded, but you're still alone too much of the time.

John 16:33 is the verse we have talked about often in this book: "In this world, you will have trouble. But take heart! I have overcome the world."

Let's look at what was going on in this verse. Jesus had just told the disciples He was about to leave them. He was their best, most trusted friend. They believed He had come to save the world, and now He was leaving. Not only was He leaving them, but He was leaving them to do the work that He had started. They weren't expecting this kind of trouble. It was all just too much. Too much of being left and too much pressure. I would guess that they felt unsure, awkward, and alone and maybe more than a little worried.

"In this world, you will have trouble," He still said. "But take heart! I have overcome the world."

I want you to expect trouble and worry. Wherever you are now, in whatever the next stage of life is. He says those very words to you now, in your room, as you're reading this book. "In this world, YOU will have trouble." In fact, He already knows the trouble you're experiencing with friends, with family, and within yourself. You will have trouble. Expect it.

In fact, I'm going to make my own list of things that I want you to expect.

You're going to have trouble with friends. Some girls can be, as you know, quite fickle. You'll have some friends off and on throughout your lifetime who won't be true friends. Fickle girls turn into fickle women. But expect to find a handful of trusted, safe friends along the way. They may come at unexpected times and in unexpected places. Those friendships will take work. Look for them and put in the work to keep them.

You will have to go it alone sometimes. Even with a great group of friends, a great husband, and your family. You are still going to feel alone at times. There is not one person—friend or husband or child—who will ever completely fulfill you. Only Jesus can do that. You can have a wonderful marriage—which also will require work. You can have some amazing children—who will make you want to lose your mind at times. You can expect trouble in your family life too—even the most connected, perfect-looking families have trouble.

I want you to expect trouble. But there are other things you can expect too—things that I told your parents about in their book. But I want you to know them even more.

> You will have good friends along the way, although they may not be the most popular friends.
>
> Kindness is more important than cool in a friend every time.
>
> Even the best of friends will hurt your feelings and leave you out sometimes.
>
> Learning how to handle conflict is more important than having a friendship where there isn't any.
>
> Every important relationship in your life will be hard sometimes.
>
> You won't be invited to every birthday party.
>
> Just because you're not someone's best friend doesn't mean you're not still a friend. Everyone has a closest few.
>
> People can still really love you and hurt your feelings, even at the same time.
>
> There is no perfect friend.
>
> There is no perfect guy.
>
> There is certainly no perfect teenage boy.
>
> Every college student feels lonely, thinks they chose the wrong college, and wishes they could transfer sometimes.
>
> There is no perfect marriage.
>
> Every job has hard days when you wish you had chosen something else.
>
> Parenting is hard. You will love your kids like crazy, and you will be glad when summer break is over.
>
> Through every stage of your life, you will worry at times. You'll worry about the things and people that are most important to you, and sometimes you'll worry about things that don't even matter.
>
> You will feel sad and angry and hurt often. Daily. But those feelings do not define you. You get to pick what defines you.

You'll never feel 100 percent confident.

You can feel courageous and fearful at the same time.

You will fail. And fail in big and little ways a million times over the course of your life.

Your failure does not define you either.

You'll often feel like something is wrong with you. You'll feel like you're the only one who _____ or who doesn't _____. You're not. And it's not.

You are exactly whom God meant for you to be, even though you won't feel like it most of the time.

In this world, you will have trouble and have it a lot.

But you can always have hope because of Jesus.

Jesus is the one friend who will never disappoint you or let you down.[1]

In this world, you will have trouble. *But . . .*

The verse doesn't stop with trouble. There is a *but*. Thank heavens, there's a *but*.

Romans 5:3–5 says it this way: "Not only so, but we also glory in our sufferings, because we know that suffering produces perseverance; perseverance, character; and character, hope. And hope does not put us to shame, because God's love has been poured out into our hearts through the Holy Spirit, who has been given to us."

"But" and "Not only so" are awfully similar in these two verses. Trouble is not where things end. In this world, we will have trouble and suffering both, but suffering produces good things. In fact, let's do a little experiment. *I want you to walk out this verse with a real-life example. Start with suffering. Actually, I can start with my example. Then you can add yours.*

A time I suffered: <u>When my parents divorced.</u>

It taught me perseverance: <u>I had never been through anything that hard. I learned that I could get through it and still be okay. That I could persevere.</u>

It grew character in me: I realized I was stronger than I knew. It helped me develop more grit.

It brought hope: Now I help kids every day whose parents are getting divorced or who are going through some type of pain. I'm better able to help because I know what it feels like to hurt in that way.

Your turn.
A time I suffered:

It taught me perseverance:

It grew character in me:

It brought hope:

Again, science backs up Scripture. There are good things happening when we struggle, even if we don't know it at the time. Research says that up to 70 percent of people who go through trauma experience profound positive transformation.[2] Experiencing difficulty grows more "grit and perseverance" in you, according to two psychologists I respect.[3] I would imagine you have certainly grown more grit and perseverance as a result of the trauma or trouble you've experienced. You've likely developed more character and hope too.

In this world, you will have trouble. But the *but* is coming. It's coming and for one reason only: grace. My favorite author, Frederick Buechner, defines grace in this way: "Here is your life. You might never have been, but you are, because the party wouldn't have been complete without you. Here is the world. Beautiful and terrible things will happen. Don't be afraid. I am with you. Nothing can ever separate us. It's for you I created the universe. I love you."[4]

In this world, we will have trouble and worries. But He has overcome the world, and in that we can certainly take heart.

A Few *Brave* Things to Remember

- In this world, we will have trouble.

- Expect trouble and expect worry.

- Sometimes our anxiety is related to our unrealistic expectations—for others, for ourselves, and for the world. When we experience trouble, we think something is wrong with us or wrong with our lives.

- Suffering produces perseverance. Perseverance produces character, and character, hope. In other words, suffering eventually creates good things in all of us.

- Science backs up this truth with research that says trauma actually grows more grit and perseverance.

8. Take Heart

So far it sounds kind of tough to be a teenage girl. Have you picked up on that?

Here's what we've established:

- You live with pressure to get things right, to succeed, to look beautiful, and to have all of your friends and followers on social media respond.
- When something goes wrong in a boy's world, he blames someone else. When something goes wrong in a girl's world, she blames herself.
- Girls tend to blame themselves for things that are either out of their control or that aren't blameworthy to begin with.
- You have changes going on in your body that create a lot of emotional upheaval.
- You have changes going on in your brain that cause your memory to falter and your confidence to dip.
- Girls often don't let themselves feel angry, disappointed, or any emotion that others might interpret as them not being kind or good or likable.

- Girls often lose their voice as they approach puberty, letting others think and problem-solve for them.
- Girls are twice as likely to struggle with worry and anxiety as boys.

Trouble. And here I am telling you to take heart. Well, really, here Jesus is.

Taking Heart or Taking Shame?

I want to add something else to the mix. You might have picked up on the fact that I often speak at parenting seminars. Most of the time, I go with this guy named David, who has worked with me for twenty-five years and is like a brother to me. We have fun going back and forth when we speak. He talks about boys. I talk about girls. Because he works mostly with boys, and I work mostly with girls. (Which means my job is way more fun. Can you imagine trying to counsel a teenage boy and get him to talk?)

Anyway, we have this class we teach called Raising Boys and Girls. In it, we describe four different stages in a boy's life and in a girl's. We go back and forth—boy stage 1, girl stage 1, boy stage 2, and so on. We talk about who you are and what you need at each stage. We've literally taught this class thousands of times together at this point. There's a particular story he tells in the class that I think you'll find quite interesting.

He talks about a boy he knew who was approaching puberty. This little guy's dad came to him, before that point, and told him all of the ways his body was going to be changing in the next few years. Then he talked about one specific thing that's going to happen (which I am NOT going to write about here, because we'd both be embarrassed). This sweet dad said to his son, "And whenever that happens, I want you to wake me up. I don't care if it's the middle of the night, because I want to be excited with you. Then

I'm going to take you out for a steak dinner, and we're going to celebrate the fact that God is making you into a man."

Don't you love that story? What a cool dad! And I'm curious what it makes you think about you.

One day, after David and I had finished teaching our class, a woman came up and said, "I want to tell you a story. I've heard David talk before," she said. "In fact, I've heard him tell that story about the dad who took his son out for a steak dinner. I decided I wanted to try it with my daughter." *Uh-oh.* You can imagine where this is going. She said, "So I told her all about her period and the changes that were going to take place in her body. I said, 'And honey, when that happens, we're going to go shopping. Because I want to celebrate with you that God is making you into a woman.'" "Really, Mom?" her daughter asked. "We're going to celebrate the fact that I'm bleeding?"

And there it is. I think something about her statement reflects something that happens inside a lot of us.

How do you feel about becoming a woman?
What does the word woman *mean to you?*

_____

_____

_____

_____

_____

I asked my high school girls' groups the same question. Do you know what their answers were?

"Uhhhhh."

"We're not sure."

"I know I'm excited to be a mom."

"I don't mean this in a sarcastic way, but can you tell me what we are supposed to be looking forward to about becoming women?"

It's a great question and one that I think is VERY important for us to talk about. Boys have a lot of eager anticipation about becoming men. It sounds cool to them. Being a man sounds strong and brave and like there should be this fierce, booming background music.

But for some of us, when we think about becoming women, we don't know exactly how we feel about it. Maybe it sounds good, but it also sounds a little uncomfortable. What does it mean we get to do? Become moms, for one thing, which sounds really great. But what if you're not a mom someday?

I believe it's kind of like starting our periods. Yes, it's a good thing, but there's this little undercurrent of shame that goes along with the idea of becoming a woman too. You might have felt it. You might still feel it. I just don't think we live with this anticipation of how amazing it's going to be when we become women. There's certainly no background music that goes with it. My hope is that we can change that. My hope is that we can have fierce (and at the same time lovely) music playing in the background too. That you would look forward with anticipation to becoming a woman. And I have a feeling that your moms and grandmothers and aunts and all of the other women in your life would want the same thing for you.

Why do you think there might be shame attached to the idea of becoming a woman?

Listen to this verse from the Psalms:

May our sons in their youth be like plants full grown, our daughters like corner pillars cut for the structure of a palace.

Psalm 144:12 ESV

I don't know about you, but I'd WAY rather be a pillar than a plant. Pillars in a palace are beautiful, first of all, but they are also

strong—they are charged with holding up the entire palace. You're those things too, and I hope this book is reminding you of that. You are lovely—who God made you to be is beautiful—from the inside out. As you have heard a million times, God does not make mistakes. And there is no part of you that is one. Even if you don't like your hair, or nose, or legs. He didn't goof on that part. You are beautiful and wonderfully made.

You are STRONG too. Just look at what you've done already in this book. You've taught yourself cognitive-behavioral therapy. You're beating your Worry Whisperer right and left! You're being vulnerable and brave and fierce.

Now, let's go back to thinking about what it means to be a woman. What's the passage you hear about the most in reference to women? Yep. Proverbs 31. I've read it a million times, but today, when I read it thinking about you, something different stood out. I want you to read this passage again—the statements in parentheses are not official biblical interpretations. They're what I would want to point out if you were sitting in my office and we were reading this passage together.

> An excellent wife who can find?
> (Not quite yet for you.)

She is far more precious than jewels.

(You are far more precious than jewels.)

The heart of her husband trusts in her, and he will have no lack of gain.

(If someone is lucky enough to marry you, God has given him a tremendous gift.)

She does him good, and not harm, all the days of her life.

(She's kind and caring.)

She seeks wool and flax, and works with willing hands.

(She's tries hard, like us.)

She is like the ships of the merchant; she brings her food from afar.

(She is also taking care of her family.)

She rises while it is yet night and provides food for her household and portions for her maidens.

(She works hard taking care of her family and friends and gets up early to make sure it's all done.)

She considers a field and buys it; with the fruit of her hands she plants a vineyard.

(Now she owns property too.)

She dresses herself with strength and makes her arms strong.

(She's fierce, in a lovely kind of way.)

She perceives that her merchandise is profitable.

(She's confident.)

Her lamp does not go out at night.

(Still working hard.)

She puts her hands to the distaff, and her hands hold the spindle.

(No idea what this means. No distaffs and spindles for us.)

She opens her hand to the poor and reaches out her hands to the needy.

(She's compassionate and thoughtful in her care for others.)

She is not afraid of snow for her household, for all her household are clothed in scarlet.

(Again, taking good care of her family—and in style.)

She makes bed coverings for herself; her clothing is fine
linen and purple.
(She's creative and stylish herself.)
Her husband is known in the gates when he sits among the
elders of the land.
(She's well-known and respected, and so is her husband,
because of her.)
She makes linen garments and sells them; she delivers
sashes to the merchant.
(Now she's also a fashion designer and seamstress.)
Strength and dignity are her clothing, and she laughs at
the time to come.
(She's playful and strong and has grace.)
She opens her mouth with wisdom, and the teaching of
kindness is on her tongue.
(She's wise and kind, yet again.)
She looks well to the ways of her household and does not
eat the bread of idleness.
(She's not playing around.)
Her children rise up and call her blessed; her husband
also, and he praises her:
"Many women have done excellently, but you surpass
them all."
(Yes, she has.)
Charm is deceitful, and beauty is vain, but a woman who
fears the Lord is to be praised.
Give her of the fruit of her hands, and let her works praise
her in the gates.

Proverbs 31:11–31 ESV

Seriously? This woman is like Oprah meets the local Pottery Barn
owner meets the Anthropologie clothing designer. She's what's
called an entrepreneur in our world, meaning a hardworking, creative, smart, high-achieving businesswoman. And she's kind, while
she's at it. And she takes great care of her family and friends. She
is lovely AND fierce—just like our background music.

What do you think her background music would be? What would you want yours to be?

She is what we can look forward to about being women. God has uniquely gifted us in many ways. According to a *Psychology Today* article, women are more appreciative of beauty and excellence, are kinder by nature, treasure close relationships, and are more naturally and outwardly grateful.[1] Another study says that women are thought to be more "compassionate and empathetic" leaders.[2] Just like our Proverbs 31 friend, we can do many things at once. Think about it . . . she's a wise, thoughtful, creative, caring, strong, hardworking, doing-it-all-and-still-loved-by-her-people kind of woman. She is a pillar. I want to be her.

Quite possibly my favorite statement about her is that she can laugh at the days to come. There is so much good that God has bound up in the heart of a woman. Good that is yours now and will continue to grow as you get older. There is much to look forward to. Yes, you will have trouble, but you can take heart and laugh at the days to come. God has given you a heart that is both fierce and lovely. A heart that leads you to be pillar-like in your own way. And a heart that I know is going to make a profound difference in this world.

Taking Heart

I love this idea of taking heart. I always have. It appears several times in Scripture (including Deuteronomy 31:6 and Psalm 31:24). I think I love it because it sounds warm and strong and comforting . . . which also sounds a lot like where we're gifted as women. The root of the phrase means to have "bold and confident courage."[3] It's exactly what you've been doing throughout the pages of this book.

I don't want taking heart to sound like pressure, though. In my mind, taking heart is not a challenge you have to work hard and rise to. It means that you *get* to take this bold, courageous heart that God has *already* placed inside of you into the world. It means you *get* to be an unstoppable force against the Worry Whisperer in your life. You can do it. *God has already given you everything you need.* And I want to remind you of just a few things that you already have and that are going to be extra important for you on this journey of fighting the Worry Whisperer. In fact, in all my years of counseling girls, I would consider these the six most important things you can take on your journey. I believe these six things together are what it means for you to take heart.

Take Community

We've already established that friendships are going to be hard at times. All relationships are. But we need each other. You need community. Taking heart is much easier when you've got others who are taking heart alongside you. Talk about your worries with a friend, with your parent, with a counselor. Don't live in isolation in this fight against the Worry Whisperer. You need others who can cheer you on along the way. That's what I've had the privilege to do throughout the pages of this book. Now I want more for you. I want you to have a few trusted people— some your age, some a little farther along on the journey. But I want you to have some folks traveling with you who know you—in other words, who you have allowed to know you. They may be hard to find. Pray. Be open to who He brings. And once you find them, remember that they won't do it right sometimes. I remember a girl telling her mom in counseling, "I just want to be loved correctly." We all do. We want to be loved all the time in the ways that most feel like love to us. Jesus always will. Others won't ever get it quite right this side of heaven. But you will find a handful of people over the course of your life who will sure try. They will have the most important traits of friendship like loyalty and genuine kindness, and they will cheer you on from the sidelines. In counseling, I call them balcony friends after a book I read a long time ago that was based on Hebrews

12:1. The image is that we've got this group of people—people on earth and people in heaven—who are cheering us on along the way. We also have basement friends, who are trying to grab our ankles as we run, tripping us up. And as one girl your age said, we have roller coaster friends. Up and down. Up and down. You know the type.

What about you? Who are the basement friends in your life right now? Roller coaster? Balcony?

Basement Friends	Coaster Friends	Balcony Friends

You'll always have a few roller coaster friends. But the balcony friends are the ones who count. They're the ones I'm talking about who are cheering you on. Who are taking heart right alongside you in their own journeys. With whom you can share your worries, and who will also bring you back to a place of truth. That's what community—real community—is. And you only need a few heart-taking balcony friends to make up community.

Take Truth

In case you haven't noticed, your emotions are going to be all over the place during these years. Your confidence will be too. You will feel tossed about like a little ship on a big ocean. When that happens, two things are important.

1) You talk to a trusted one or two or few—your community.
2) You always go back to a place of truth.

If you've ever wondered what it would be like to be a counselor, that's it. That's what I do every day. I get to hang out with girls and (1) hear them share their hearts and their worries and (2) help them go back to a place of truth. That truth is like an anchor. In fact, Hebrews 6:19 says, "We have this hope as an anchor for the soul, firm and secure." The hope this verse is referring to is God's promise, His Word.

You are going to feel a million feelings in a day, maybe even an hour. I hope that you do. I want you to allow all of those feelings to bubble up inside of you. They're what make you as passionate as you are. But just because you feel something doesn't mean it's truth. Your feelings can stir the Worry Whisperer up. It can quickly shift from "That hurt to see my friends together on social media when I wasn't invited" to "They don't want me there" to "They don't even want to be my friends anymore" to "I don't have any friends." Feelings can turn into untruths very quickly. We won't say lies, really . . . they're more like imaginings, as a friend of mine calls them. It's imagining based on what worry is whispering in that moment. Then our emotions get even more stirred up because we're interpreting those imaginings as truth. Our cortex is scaring our amygdala, to go back to Anxiety Brain 101.

Let yourself feel. Talk about it. Journal. Paint or draw. As we talked about, those feelings need to come out. But then I want you to go back to a place of truth. This is where friends come in. Or your mom. Or someone like me. You want someone who will listen first, and then say, "Now tell me what is true." In the above scenario, the truth might be, "Well, I might not be their first friend. But I know they invite me sometimes. I have other first friends. Ella always invites me. She is my balcony friend. And I'm certain that Jesus loves me always. He's sure chosen me." Truth. Truth comforts us and helps us have courage. Truth helps us take heart.

My favorite truths are verses I love. Sometimes, when I can't think of anything else true, I'll go back to those, whether they're about worry or about how much God loves me. The Bible, as you might remember from Sunday school, is called a sword several times in Scripture. Hebrews 4:12 says, "For the word of God is living and active, sharper than any two-edged sword, piercing to the division of soul and of spirit, of joints and of marrow, and discerning the thoughts and intentions of the heart" (ESV). In *The Message*, it says, "Nothing and no one is impervious to God's Word. We can't get away from it—no matter what." That *nothing* and *no one* includes the Worry Whisperer. Hymns and worship songs help me too, as they're filled with rich truth.

We all need truth. My friend David says that feelings are like little children. You don't want to stuff them in the trunk (ignored), but you don't want to let them drive the car either. The safest place for them to be is strapped into the back seat. Truth helps you do that. Your emotions are important, but they don't have the most power. Truth does. Next time your feelings are swirling about and dragging you around with them, anchor yourself with truth. *What are three truths you can go back to right now? They can be about you or about something you've learned from God's Word that feels especially important today.*

Great job! Continue to take truth with you as an anchor on this journey. It will strengthen your faith, and it will strengthen that lovely, fierce heart of yours too.

Take Gratitude

Hopetown has to be one of the most grateful places in the world. It's probably our most important rule with the kids, other than being kind. Whether it's someone who's cooked you a meal or pulled you behind a boat on a tube or let you go before them to get dinner, we say "thank you" constantly. Years and years ago, someone told me something I'll never forget: "Satan can't live in a thankful heart." Let's go back to our secret name for the Worry Whisperer. Yep. There's an anchoring truth for you. The Worry Whisperer is stripped of his power when your heart is full of gratitude. In fact, that's something I read in my research too—gratitude and worry cannot coexist. It's impossible. You can't be anxious and grateful at the same time. Try it. It's one or the other.

And get this: Gratitude produces more serotonin in your brain, which, you remember, is referred to as the "happy chemical." Serotonin elevates your mood, reduces depression, and regulates anxiety.

What are five things you're grateful for right now?

I know friends who practice gratitude together, reminding each other of what they're grateful for. I know families who practice gratitude around the dinner table. I also know girls your age who have entire journals devoted to gratitude, practicing a little each

169

day. *Practice* is an important word here. Gratitude isn't the natural inclination of our hearts—most of us don't wake up grateful in the morning. But we get better at what we practice. Practice gratitude. It will be important in your fight against the Worry Whisperer. It will help you feel better and take heart. I believe that gratitude not only helps us in the moment, but transforms us into more grateful and less anxious people.

Take Purpose

Do you remember our verse from 1 John? It's another truth I anchor to regularly.

> My dear children, let's not just talk about love; let's practice real love. This is the only way we'll know we're living truly, living in God's reality. It's also the way to shut down debilitating self-criticism, even when there is something to it. For God is greater than our worried hearts and knows more about us than we do ourselves.
>
> 1 John 3:18–20 THE MESSAGE

Debilitating self-criticism, if you remember, is one of the ways the Worry Whisperer loves to come after us, making us criticize and get angry at ourselves. *"That was stupid." "Why did you say that?" "I'm sure they thought you were weird." "You blew that one."*

First John 3 says that *the way to shut down debilitating self-criticism is to love.* Purpose. It's that simple. When we are thinking about giving to someone else, we can't really think about ourselves. It's no longer about us and our failures. It's about the other person.

Purpose changes us too—like gratitude. It can also anchor us. It sure anchors me. When I feel hurt or angry or I'm overwhelmed by something going on in my life, I will often ask myself one question: "Who do I want to be in this?" or even "Who do I believe God has called me to be?" Those questions pull me out of the waves of feeling and take me back to a place of truth. And the answer, most often, is that He has called me to love. It's a really great cycle. If I love someone else by giving to them or helping them when I'm feeling bad about myself, it's actually the thing that helps me feel the best about myself. Purpose.

I want you to take purpose. I want you to know that God has called you to love. He has called you to so many good things that only you can do.

Take YOU. YOUR Heart.

As we talked about before, it's easy to fade in these years. You likely will a little. But I don't want you to disappear. I want this journey to be about two things—no, three. The first is learning how to fight your Worry Whisperer. The second is learning how to be more fully you. And the third—well, we'll get to that one in a minute.

When I was little, I loved to have friends over. But after we'd played for a few hours, I'd quietly go find my mom and say, "Mommy, it's been so fun playing with _____. But when are they going home?"

I think part of it was because I was tired. I was tired of having to make sure that they were having fun. But another part of it was I was an introvert and needed time by myself to recharge. I had no idea what that meant at the time. I used to think how I felt was more about the other person and how they were "getting on my nerves" than it was about me. Now looking back, I see that it was all about me. As an adult, I'm still learning that when I get tired and grumpy, it's an oil light for me. What I thought was a problem was really just a part of my personality. And that's okay. It's not that I'm grumpy—or the other person is annoying—I just need a few minutes to myself from time to time. It's not selfish. It's not unkind. It helps me be a better version of myself.

We live in that balance of purpose and of knowing and doing the things that refill us to take us back to a place of purpose. You already know some of the things that refill you—God's Word, prayer, worship. Those fill all of our hearts in a way that enables us to return to loving others, to purpose. But there are going to be some additional specific things that refill you. Maybe it's art. Maybe it's running. Maybe it's reading. Maybe it's time by yourself. Maybe it's time with balcony friends.

What are five things that help you be a better version of yourself?

_____

_____

_____

_____

_____

This journey of taking heart, of fighting your Worry Whisperer, of discovering you is going to start with you. Understanding more of who you are certainly helps you understand who you're becoming. I'd recommend checking out the Enneagram too. It has helped me understand myself and others better than any tool I've come across in my lifetime. There are some great books by an author named Suzanne Stabile that can help. It's much easier to take heart when you know your heart. And knowing your heart is where your journey begins. Let's jump to the end, to that last thing this journey is really about.

Learning to fight your Worry Whisperer.
Learning how to be more fully you.
Learning to trust.

Take Trust

The last thing I want to mention is something you may feel like you have trouble with. I talk to girls your age every day who say trust is a hard concept for them. I know . . . you've been let down. I know . . . you're not sure who you can trust. Let me assure you that you can *always* trust Jesus. When it comes down to it,

His love and grace for us are the only reasons we can take heart. He has overcome the world and every Worry Whisperer that has ever been or ever will be. That is why we can take heart. In this world, we will have trouble, but we can take heart *because* He has overcome the world. Keep reading. You've got this, because He's got you. That is certainly something you can trust.

A Few *Brave* Things to Remember

- In this world, you will have trouble, but you can take heart.

- Sometimes, girls take more shame than they do heart. That shame can impact your view of what it means to become a woman.

- God has gifted us, as women, with a unique ability to be both lovely and fierce at the same time. He has given you a strong, brave, lovely, fierce heart that He wants you to take out into the world.

- Taking heart involves taking community. You need other women who are taking heart alongside you and reminding you of how brave you are.

- Taking truth is foundationally important to the journey. Your feelings and the Worry Whisperer are going to try to tell you what's true about your life. But only you and God get to do that. Anchor yourself to truth—His truth.

- Gratitude and worry cannot coexist. Practice gratitude.

- God has given you a unique purpose in this world—not just for when you're an adult, but for today. Purpose shuts down our self-criticism and changes us.

- Take your heart. God calls you to be fully you.

9. He Has Overcome

> God has not given us a spirit of fear, but of power and
> of love and of a sound mind.
>
> 2 Timothy 1:7 NKJV

> He saved us . . . not because of anything we have done
> but because of his own purpose and grace.
>
> 2 Timothy 1:9

In this world, we will have trouble, but we can take heart because He has overcome the world. For His own purpose and by His own grace.

For His Purpose

God wants to use you. I hope you've heard that strongly throughout the pages of this book. He has a job for you that only you can do. Actually, He has a million jobs for you through the rest of your life, in daily ways and big-picture ways. It may be that you're a mom. It may be that you're a writer. It may be that you're a counselor, like me. It may be that you're the president. But He has a job that He specifically created just for you. Even with your failures, insecurities, and worries. He has called you as exactly who He has made you to be.

By His Grace

That might be my favorite part of this verse. "Not because of anything we ourselves have done." I know that you're a "try hard-er" like me. It's one of the reasons I know we'd be friends. But this battle, this journey, is by His grace. No trying hard needed. You can rest in His grace.

Matthew 11:28–30 in *The Message* says, "Are you tired? Worn out? Burned out on religion? Come to me. Get away with me and you'll recover your life. I'll show you how to take a real rest. Walk with me and work with me—watch how I do it. Learn the unforced rhythms of grace. I won't lay anything heavy or ill-fitting on you. Keep company with me and you'll learn to live freely and lightly."

With Practice

Yes, I still want you to practice. Rest and practice. Just like He says, "Walk with me and work with me—watch how I do it." Rest knowing that He's already won the battle. You're still fighting, but you're fighting under this banner of grace. Remember, the number one reason any of us don't beat the Worry Whisperer is because we forget to practice. You'll blow it when you're practicing. You'll gain some ground. And then you'll blow it again. Keep on practicing. Keep on fighting, knowing that God has already gone before you and won.

Knowing Freedom

We've talked about a lot of things in this book, but there is one very important thing I've forgotten to say: Courage doesn't exist in the absence of fear, but rather in the presence of it. What that means is what we've said over and over: The Worry Whisperer will be back. When he comes back, I don't want you to get mad at yourself and think you've failed. I want you to think, *That old Worry Whisperer is back again. He didn't beat me before, and he won't beat me this time.*

Think about some of the heroes of our faith. David (he beat Goliath), Moses (he beat lots of people whose names end with *ites*), and Samson (he beat pretty much everyone). Now think about your favorite superhero. These people became superheroes in battle, in the fight. We know who they are because they had courage in the midst of fear. They're remembered for their courage, not their fear. Your courage is the same. When those worries come, as they will, I want you to shrug your shoulders in a Peter Parker kind of way and run right back into battle. There is a whole lot of freedom in knowing the worries will come and that you can do this through His grace. And with something else that is especially important.

With Love

Have you seen the documentary *Won't You Be My Neighbor?* If not, I'd love for you to watch it in the next few weeks. Mr. Rogers was one of my favorite people when I was little and watched his TV show. And he is even more so now that I've seen that documentary. Mr. Rogers was all about making people feel loved. One of his songs reminds me of how I feel about you. In it he says, "It's you I like," not the outward things about you and "not the things that hide you."[1]

Here's the thing. It's not just how I feel about you. More than that, I believe it's how God feels about you. God loves you immensely. And He likes you. You. Not the social media version of you. Not even the try-hard version of you. Believing that, trusting that, might take the most practice and grace. My prayer would be that you would believe—all the way down to your toes—how much He likes and loves you. I'm praying that for you even as I'm writing this paragraph. He does. And that's why this entire brave journey circles back around to trust.

Taking and Living in Trust

In my research, I read that acceptance of the fact that worry will be back is the antidote to anxiety. That means it cancels anxiety out. I do think acceptance is important—which we've already established. The Worry Whisperer will be back, but every time, he'll have less and less power. And every time he returns, you'll grow stronger. You'll grow more into your super strength. You'll grow more into the fierce, lovely woman God has uniquely made you to be. Acceptance is important, but I believe the antidote to anxiety is something different.

Let me tell you why I named my dog Lucy. Have you ever seen *Prince Caspian*? Lucy is one of my favorite characters in the Chronicles of Narnia books and movies. If you haven't watched the movies, I would suggest that you do. Right now. As in, go put down this book and watch.

In *Prince Caspian*, the Telmarine army is coming against the army of Aslan. Lucy has a conversation with Aslan, the lion, who represents Jesus. Lucy is saying things like "I wish I was braver," because Lucy has a Worry Whisperer too. Aslan responds with "If you were any braver, you would be a lioness."[2] The scene cuts to Lucy walking out onto a bridge. On the other side of that bridge is the entire army Lucy and her people are fighting against. Lucy walks out by herself and pulls out a tiny knife. Immediately, Aslan walks out right beside her. He is with her.

The reason Aslan is with her is because He loves her. It's apparent when you read the book or watch the movie. And He loves you just as much, although His love for you is a special relationship between just the two of you. He likes you. He likes you enough that He didn't just defeat the Worry Whisperer—He beat death for you. You can trust that truth more than you can trust anything in your life. That trust was what enabled Lucy to walk out on the bridge against an entire army, knowing that she wasn't alone. She had Aslan.

Our Benediction

Do you know what a benediction is? It's the final truth you end a worship service with at church. Here is our benediction, the truths I want you to hold on to the most at the end of this book and our time together.

1. You're not alone in your worries.
2. Your worries don't mean something is wrong with you.
3. There is a Worry Whisperer on the prowl who wants do everything he can to keep you from discovering the you God uniquely made you to be.
4. The Worry Whisperer will come after your body, trying to set off false alarms that make you feel like you're not okay.
5. He'll come after your mind, trying to make you think that the problem is bigger than you are.
6. He'll come after your heart, trying to take away every feeling you have except worry and sending the message that you can't do it—whatever "it" happens to be.
7. But here's the truth: You can.
8. In this world, you will have trouble, but you can take heart because Jesus has overcome. You can take trust and community and gratitude and truth and live in the purpose God has called YOU to. His purpose. By His grace and love.

God walks out into the fight against the Worry Whisperer beside you. I have a feeling that He'd come to where you're standing on the bridge and stop right beside you. In that moment, the little bitty knife in your hand would feel like a giant sword. Then He'd put His enormous paw—or hand—on your back and smile. He'd call you by name and say, "You are bigger than any worry that will ever come your way. You're not defined by your worries or your anxiety. You're not defined by your struggles. You are defined by my love and this fierce, lovely heart that you get to take out into the world. I'm with you."

> The LORD bless you and keep you; the LORD make his face shine on you and be gracious to you; the LORD turn his face toward you and give you peace.

> Numbers 6:24–26

Now, go get that Worry Whisperer.

A Few *Brave* Things to Remember

- God has called you for His own purpose and by His own grace (2 Timothy 1:9).

- God wants to use you. He has a job for you that only you can do.

- That job is not pressure. It's by His grace. You can rest knowing He's already won the battle against any Worry Whisperer that could ever come your way.

- Courage doesn't exist in the absence of fear, but in the presence of it.

- God loves you and likes you. The real you. That's why you can trust, and that trust is the only real antidote to anxiety.

- In this world you will have trouble, but you can take heart because the God who likes and loves you has overcome the world.

Notes

To the Parent Who Bought This Book

1. Reid Wilson and Lynn Lyons, *Anxious Kids, Anxious Parents: 7 Ways to Stop the Worry Cycle and Raise Courageous & Independent Children* (Deerfield Beach, FL: Health Communications, 2013), 26.

2. Perri Klass, "How to Help a Child With an Anxiety Disorder," *New York Times*, October 1, 2018, https://www.nytimes.com/2018/10/01/well/family/how-to-help-a-child-with-an-anxiety-disorder.html.

3. David A. Clark and Aaron T. Beck, *Anxiety and Worry Workbook: The Cognitive Behavioral Solution* (New York: The Guilford Press, 2012), 41, 51.

4. Sissy Goff, *Raising Worry-Free Girls: Helping Your Daughter Feel Braver, Stronger, and Smarter in an Anxious World* (Minneapolis: Bethany House, 2019), 31.

Introduction

1. "Any Anxiety Disorder," National Institute of Mental Health, November 2017 update, https://www.nimh.nih.gov/health/statistics/any-anxiety-disorder.shtml.

Chapter 1: Defining the Worry Words

1. "Any Anxiety Disorder," National Institute of Mental Health, November 2017 update, https://www.nimh.nih.gov/health/statistics/any-anxiety-disorder.shtml.

2. Ron Steingard, "Mood Disorders and Teenage Girls," Child Mind Institute, accessed August 12, 2020, https://childmind.org/article/mood-disorders-and-teenage-girls/.

3. C. S. Lewis, *The Four Loves* (New York: HarperCollins, 1960), 83.

4. Tamar Chansky, "Welcome to Worrywisekids," the Children's and Adult Center for OCD and Anxiety, accessed April 25, 2019, http://www.worrywisekids.org.

Chapter 2: Why Me?

1. Reid Wilson and Lynn Lyons, *Anxious Kids, Anxious Parents: 7 Ways to Stop the Worry Cycle and Raise Courageous & Independent Children* (Deerfield Beach, FL: Health Communications, 2013), 26.

2. "Children and Trauma," produced by the 2008 Presidential Task Force on Posttraumatic Stress Disorder and Trauma in Children and Adolescents, American Psychological Association, 2011, https://www.apa.org/pi/families/resources/children-trauma-update.

3. "Children and Trauma," 2008 Presidential Task Force, https://www.apa.org/pi/families/resources/children-trauma-update.

4. Jean Twenge, Gabrielle Martin, and W. Keith Campbell, "Decreases in Psychological Well-Being among American Adolescents after 2012 and Links to Screen Time During the Rise of Smartphone Technology," *Emotion* 18, no. 6 (September 2018): 765–780, accessed at APA PsycNet, https://psycnet.apa.org/doiLanding?doi=10.1037%2Femo0000403.

5. Anya Kamanetz, "The Scientific Debate Over Teens, Screens and Mental Health," *Life Kit* podcast, NPR.org, August 27, 2019, https://www.npr.org/2019/08/27/754362629/the-scientific-debate-over-teens-screens-and-mental-health.

6. Elizabeth Hoge, David Bickham, and Joanne Cantor, "Digital Media, Anxiety, and Depression in Children," *Pediatrics* 140, no. Supplement 2 (November 2017), https://pediatrics.aappublications.org/content/140/Supplement_2/S76.

7. NIH/National Institute of Mental Health, "Infant Temperament Predicts Personality More than 20 Years Later," *ScienceDaily*, April 20, 2020, www.sciencedaily.com/releases/2020/04/200420201513.htm.

8. Claire Shipman, Katty Kay, and Jillellyn Riley, "How Puberty Kills Girls' Confidence," *Atlantic*, September 20, 2018, https://www.theatlantic.com/family/archive/2018/09/puberty-girls-confidence/563804/.

9. Melissa Trevathan and Sissy Goff, *Raising Girls* (Grand Rapids, MI: Zondervan, 2007), 75–76.

10. Sissy Goff, *Raising Worry-Free Girls: Helping Your Daughter Feel Braver, Stronger, and Smarter in an Anxious World* (Minneapolis: Bethany House, 2019), 31.

Chapter 3: How Will This Help?

1. David A. Clark and Aaron T. Beck, *Anxiety and Worry Workbook: The Cognitive Behavioral Solution* (New York: The Guilford Press, 2012), 41, 51.

2. Dan B. Allender, *The Healing Path: How the Hurts in Your Past Can Lead You to a More Abundant Life* (Colorado Springs: WaterBrook, 1999), 189.

3. Robert Frost, "The Road Not Taken" in *Complete Poems of Robert Frost* (New York: Holt, Rinehart, and Winston, 1949), 131.

4. Bridgett Flynn Walker, *Anxiety Relief for Kids: On-the-Spot Strategies to Help Your Child Overcome Worry, Panic & Avoidance* (Oakland, CA: New Harbinger Publications, 2017), 20.

Chapter 4: Help for Your Body

1. Catherine Pittman, "Rewire the Anxious Brain: Using Neuroscience to End Anxiety, Panic and Worry," March 13, 2017, a PESI digital seminar, https://catalog.pesi.com/item/19659/?_ga=2.223424467.918260906.1591987936-1079570723.1539110393.

2. Robert M. Sapolsky, "How to Relieve Stress," *Greater Good*, University of California, Berkeley, March 22, 2012, https://greatergood.berkeley.edu/article/item/how_to_relieve_stress.

3. Daniel J. Siegel and Tina Payne Bryson, *The Yes Brain: How to Cultivate Courage, Curiosity, and Resilience in Your Child* (New York: Bantam Books, 2018), 17.

4. William Stixrud and Ned Johnson, *The Self-Driven Child: The Science and Sense of Giving Your Kids More Control Over Their Lives* (New York: Viking, 2018), 23.

5. Arlin Cuncic, "Amygdala Hijack and the Fight or Flight Response," Verywell Mind, accessed August 12, 2020, https://www.verywellmind.com/what-happens-during-an-amygdala-hijack-4165944.

6. Pittman, "Rewire the Anxious Brain."

7. Philippians 4:8 NKJV.

8. Sue McGreevey, "Eight Weeks to a Better Brain," *Harvard Gazette*, January 21, 2011, https://news.harvard.edu/gazette/story/2011/01/eight-weeks-to-a-better-brain/.

9. James Lake, "How Exercise Reduces Anxiety," *Psychology Today*, October 16, 2018, https://www.psychologytoday.com/us/blog/integrative-mental-health-care/201810/how-exercise-reduces-anxiety.

10. "Sleep Disorders," Anxiety and Depression Association of America, accessed July 15, 2020, https://adaa.org/understanding-anxiety/related-illnesses/sleep-disorders.

11. Jodi A. Mindell and Judith A. Owens, *A Clinical Guide to Pediatric Sleep: Diagnosis and Management of Sleep Problems* (Philadelphia: Lippincott Williams & Wilkins, 2003), 36.

12. Daniel J. Siegel and Tina Payne Bryson, *The Yes Brain: How to Cultivate Courage, Curiosity, and Resilience in Your Child* (New York: Bantam Books, 2018), 62.

13. Dan Siegel, quoted by Fiona MacDonald, "Here's What Happens to Your Body When You Check Your Smartphone Before Bed," Science Alert, July 29, 2015, https://www.sciencealert.com/watch-here-s-what-happens-to-your-body-when-you-check-your-smartphone-before-bed.

14. David Rock, "Announcing the Healthy Mind Platter," *Psychology Today*, June 2, 2011, https://www.psychologytoday.com/us/blog/your-brain-work/201106/announcing-the-healthy-mind-platter.

15. Sissy Goff, *Raising Worry-Free Girls: Helping Your Daughter Feel Braver, Stronger, and Smarter in an Anxious World* (Minneapolis: Bethany House, 2019), 101–103.

Chapter 5: Help for Your Mind

1. Jena E. Pincott, "Wicked Thoughts," *Psychology Today*, September 1, 2015, https://www.psychologytoday.com/us/articles/201509/wicked-thoughts.

2. Claire Shipman, Katty Kay, and Jillellyn Riley, "How Puberty Kills Girls' Confidence," *Atlantic*, September 20, 2018, https://www.theatlantic.com/family/archive/2018/09/puberty-girls-confidence/563804/.

3. Rachel Simmons, "Ready to Stop Overthinking? Try This Simple, 4-Step Process," accessed August 6, 2020, https://www.rachelsimmons.com/stop-over thinking/.

4. Louisa C. Michl et al., "Rumination as a Mechanism Linking Stressful Life Events to Symptoms of Depression and Anxiety: Longitudinal Evidence in Early Adolescents and Adults," *Journal of Abnormal Psychology* 122, no. 2 (May 2013): 339–352, https://www.ncbi.nlm.nih.gov/pmc/articles/PMC4116082/.

5. "Someone to Complain with Isn't Necessarily a Good Thing, Especially for Teenage Girls," American Psychological Association, accessed August 6, 2020, https://www.apa.org/news/press/releases/2007/07/co-rumination.

6. Cathy Creswell, Monika Parkinson, Kerstin Thirlwall, and Lucy Willetts, *Parent-Led CBT for Child Anxiety: Helping Parents Help Their Kids* (New York: The Guilford Press, 2017), 42.

7. Catherine Pittman, "Rewire the Anxious Brain: Using Neuroscience to End Anxiety, Panic and Worry," March 13, 2017, a PESI digital seminar, https://catalog.pesi .com/item/19659/?_ga=2.223424467.918260906.1591987936-1079570723.1539110393.

Chapter 6: Help for Your Heart

1. Dan B. Allender, *The Healing Path: How the Hurts in Your Past Can Lead You to a More Abundant Life* (Colorado Springs: WaterBrook, 1999), 189.

2. Reid Wilson and Lynn Lyons, *Anxious Kids, Anxious Parents: 7 Ways to Stop the Worry Cycle and Raise Courageous and Independent Children* (Deerfield Beach, FL: Health Communications, 2013), 16.

3. Neel Burton, "What Are Basic Emotions?" *Psychology Today*, January 7, 2016, https://www.psychologytoday.com/us/blog/hide-and-seek/201601/what-are-basic -emotions.

4. "All Human Behaviour Can Be Reduced to 'Four Basic Emotions,'" *BBC News*, February 3, 2014, https://www.bbc.com/news/uk-scotland-glasgow-west-26019586.

5. *Inside Out*, directed by Pete Docter and Ronnie del Carmen, produced by Jonas Rivera (Emeryville, CA: Pixar Animation Studios, 2015), DVD.

6. University of California–Los Angeles, "Putting Feelings into Words Produces Therapeutic Effects in the Brain," *ScienceDaily*, June 22, 2007, https://www.science daily.com/releases/2007/06/070622090727.htm.

7. Catherine Pittman, "Rewire the Anxious Brain: Using Neuroscience to End Anxiety, Panic and Worry," March 13, 2017, a PESI digital seminar, https://catalog .pesi.com/item/19659/?_ga=2.223424467.918260906.1591987936-1079570723.153 9110393.

8. Wilson and Lyons, *Anxious Kids, Anxious Parents*, 102.

Chapter 7: Trouble

1. Sissy Goff, *Raising Worry-Free Girls: Helping Your Daughter Feel Braver, Stronger, and Smarter in an Anxious World* (Minneapolis: Bethany House, 2019), 172–173.

2. Daniel J. Siegel and Tina Payne Bryson, *The Yes Brain: How to Cultivate Courage, Curiosity, and Resilience in Your Child* (New York: Bantam Books, 2018), 120.

3. Siegel and Bryson, *The Yes Brain*, 82.

4. Frederick Buechner, *Beyond Words: Daily Readings in the ABC's of Faith* (New York: HarperCollins, 2004), 139.

Chapter 8: Take Heart

1. Ryan M. Niemiec, "Women are Higher Than Men on These 4 Strengths," *Psychology Today*, April 24, 2018, https://www.psychologytoday.com/us/blog/what-matters-most/201804/women-are-higher-men-these-4-strengths.

2. Juliana Menasce Horowitz, Ruth Igielnik, and Kim Parker, "Views on Leadership Traits and Competencies and How They Intersect with Gender," *Women and Leadership 2018*, Pew Research Center, September 20, 2018, https://www.pewsocialtrends.org/2018/09/20/2-views-on-leadership-traits-and-competencies-and-how-they-intersect-with-gender/.

3. Amber C. Haines, "What It Means to Take Heart, Part 2," *(in)courage*, accessed August 6, 2020, https://www.incourage.me/2013/08/what-it-means-to-take-heart-part-2.html.

Chapter 9: He Has Overcome

1. "It's You I Like," by Fred Rogers, track 8 on *You Are Special*, Omnivore Recordings, 2020, compact disc.

2. *The Chronicles of Narnia: Prince Caspian*, directed by Andrew Adamson (Burbank, CA: Walt Disney Home Entertainment, 2008), DVD.

About the Author

Sissy Goff, MEd, LPC-MHSP, is the director of child and adolescent counseling at Daystar Counseling Ministries in Nashville, Tennessee, where she works alongside her counseling assistant/pet therapist, Lucy the Havanese. Since 1993, Sissy has been helping girls and their parents find confidence in who they are and hope in who God is making them to be, both as individuals and families. She is the author of several books, including the bestselling *Raising Worry-Free Girls*, and a sought-after speaker for parenting events.

The Feelings Chart for www.raisingboysandgirls.com by *Katie Plunkett*